Mindful Colouring

Mindful Colouring

Recovery Stories from Disordered Eating

Dr. Michèle Laliberté
PSYCHOLOGIST

Sharon Trottier
ART THERAPIST

Rock's Mills Press
2018

PUBLISHED BY
Rock's Mills Press

Copyright © 2018 by Michèle Laliberté and Sharon Trottier
All rights reserved. Published by arrangement with the authors.

For information, including Library and Archives Canada CIP data, please contact:
customer.service@rocksmillspress.com

Contents

Each Recovery Theme begins with "A Therapist's Perspective," followed by "A Patient's Perspective" and "My Recovery Story." Notes on the artwork and the artwork inspired by that recovery story immediately follow.

INTRODUCTION

This book was initially Sharon's idea. She approached me because she was interested in creating a colouring book for people recovering from an eating disorder. As a person who had recovered from an eating disorder herself, and as an artist, she wanted to "give back" and help others find their way to wellness. I thought it was an excellent idea. For my part, I had always wanted to put a book together of recovery stories. As a therapist, I often tell the people I work with stories of others who've come before them; stories that I hope will inspire them when they are scared or disappointed in themselves; stories of people who have made it through similarly difficult times and have continued on to recover from their eating disorder. As a book intended to help you through the difficult times of recovery, we wanted to provide you with a distress tolerance tool— the pages for you to colour. The stories of those who have recovered, we hope, will provide you with reassurance and inspiration.

The people who have contributed their stories were patients at the eating disorders program at St. Joseph's Healthcare in Hamilton, Ontario. A few were patients in my private practice. Their stories tell of recovery from many different types of disordered eating: anorexia nervosa, bulimia nervosa, binge eating disorder, and many other variants of an eating disorder. At the time they wrote their stories, they were at different points in recovery. Some had been recovered for years; others were barely out of treatment. Many had not had symptoms in a very long time; others were still experiencing the occasional setback. They had all worked hard at change. Each person came with a unique background that contributed to their eating disorder, and each faced different challenges as part of their recovery. They are all wonderful, and knowing them as I do, their stories fill me with joy. They chose to contribute to this book because they also wanted to "give back" and help someone earlier in the recovery process. Both Sharon and I are deeply grateful to them for participating in this book.

The book is broken down into different themes that we felt were part of the recovery process for almost everyone. For each of these themes, I have written my thoughts from the perspective of a therapist who has now been working in the field of eating disorders for over 20 years. Every theme also has been commented on by one or two people who have recovered, or are "in recovery" from an eating disorder. Each of these people then share their own recovery stories. These stories are written in their own words, and reflect the things they thought you might find helpful to hear as you work towards recovery. We hope that you will see yourself in one or more of these stories. Each person who contributed their story was asked to choose a subject for the artwork Sharon would create—something that they associated with recovery, or found soothing in times of distress. At the end of each person's story we let you know what they requested and Sharon describes what inspired her from their stories and their requests.

Before you read the recovery stories, please remember that each person has been asked to summarize their experience in relatively few words. There is so much more that they could have written, and of course, life has not ended with the story. For the majority, wellness has deepened with time. For some, wellness is something they have to keep fighting for—often because anxiety or mood makes recovery more precarious. If you read these stories and feel that your experience is so much messier, full of doubts and setbacks—well, know that their recoveries were not tidy. Every one of them struggled—and made the decision to keep going—at points in their recovery. I know, because I was there to witness the process. So, keep trying.

We hope you find this book helpful. At the end of this book, we have a place for your story, and a place for you to create your own artwork. We hope you find your way to recovery as have the others whose stories come before yours.

Michèle

ACKNOWLEDGEMENTS

We would like to thank all the wonderful individuals who contributed their stories to this book. We know they chose to participate because they hoped that their stories might help others working towards recovery from an eating disorder. We would also like to acknowledge the many individuals whose recovery stories could be included in this book—there are so many Michèle has met, and continues to meet, whose stories are uniquely inspiring. We wish the book could have gone on and on....

We would also like to thank the many clinicians from different disciplines who work with individuals with eating disorders. These clinicians have contributed to so many recovery stories that might not have happened without their dedication, caring and hard work.

We would also like to thank the families and friends whose support makes recovery possible, and worthwhile.

Finally, we would like to thank St. Josephs' Hospital for supporting the Eating Disorders Clinic. We want to specifically acknowledge the amazing staff who work in this clinic—who care deeply for the individuals to whom they provide treatment, who work to train new people in the field, and who carry out research to guide these efforts.

MICHÈLE AND SHARON

Recovery Theme 1

BEING BRAVE ENOUGH
TO TELL YOUR STORY
AND ASK FOR HELP

A Therapist's Perspective on Being Brave Enough to Tell Your Story and Ask for Help:
Michèle

One of the hardest steps in recovery from an eating disorder can be the first one: deciding to open up to someone and ask for help.

You may have felt embarrassed to admit to the behaviours that are part of your eating disorder. Perhaps you felt ashamed to be so preoccupied with weight and shape as you judge these to be superficial concerns. You maybe found it hard to admit to any area of difficulty, or to accept help from another person when you felt you should be managing the problem on your own. Perhaps most difficult for anyone with an eating disorder can be the fear that if you do seek help, the changes you will be asked to make might affect your weight and shape in a way you won't like. There are so many reasons to feel afraid…

I think this is why people are described as "brave" when they decide to seek help for an eating disorder. You may not have felt brave—you may have felt you had no choice. But the truth is that you could have kept on deciding to do nothing. It takes true courage to set out down a path where the outcome is uncertain, especially when that path is at times scary and hard.

If you have decided to start this journey, then you have already shown great courage. Eating disorders thrive in secrecy, so telling your story is such an important step towards recovery. Asking for help is not a weakness; it is being resourceful. *Have no doubt: if you recover, it is you who will have done the work and made the changes.* It is just common sense to get good information, support and strategies to help you be successful. So get the best help you can find!

A Patient's Perspective on Being Brave Enough to Tell Your Story and Ask for Help:
Katie

I never told anyone about my disorder because I was terrified that people would find out and judge me for it. I suffered in silence for over a year and a half. One day in a last ditch effort to help myself I told a "friend"; my thought was if I told them that they might be able to help in some way and I would have someone to talk to. Unfortunately, that person wasn't much of a friend and used it against me later. From that point forward it was really hard for me open up about my disorder. I didn't feel comfortable telling anyone. I felt very alone and now betrayed. I didn't know what to do. I don't have a great relationship with my mom and am not super close with my family so telling a family member was never an option for me. I do have a lot of close friends, friends I could totally tell my story to but I could never bring myself to actually do it. I was afraid that because I worked in health and wellness, it would somehow discredit me. I finally decided that I had to get help not just for me but also for my son so I went to talk to my family doctor.

When I was accepted into treatment, I was terrified. I didn't want anyone to know! But being able to talk to others who were in the same situation, having people to relate to and trust with the information I so desperately wanted to keep hidden was so liberating and freeing in itself. I can honestly say that having people to talk to about my story with no judgment was one of the keys to my recovery. To this day I have not told my family or friends but being able to be published in this book, to tell my story and implement what I have learned into my business, is very therapeutic and brings me so much joy and pleasure to be able to help others. Maybe one day I will stand up and tell my story but that needs to happen in time and when it feels right.

Andrea

Many people find it hard to disclose things about themselves or to ask for help with a problem because they fear they may be ridiculed, be viewed by others as a burden, or seen as weak. The truth is, in being afraid you assume a burden that could otherwise be easily shared and resolved with others. You also deprive those who would love you and are eager to help, the chance to assist you. Be brave, speak up. Help is just around the corner!

Katie: My Recovery Story

DIAGNOSIS: BULIMIA NERVOSA

My eating disorder started when I was 10 years old. I was in and out of my disorder and for whatever reason it didn't typically last that long. I seemed to be able to pull myself out of it. My binging and purging would resurface when I felt out of control in my life somehow, or something major had gone on. When I was 10 my mom got remarried and we moved in with my step dad. Then when I was 24, married and feeling a little lost in my relationship I began to binge and purge again. Having gone through bouts of my disorder throughout my life, I was still always able to pull myself out of it. However, the last time at age 34 I started again. I had done my first fitness competition and it was really hard for me getting back to my normal weight because it now seemed "fat" to me. Also during that same time someone who I was close with drugged me for his own personal enjoyment. It was a lot for one person to deal and cope with, let alone someone who had suffered from a past eating disorder.

I couldn't seem to get it under control. I tried so many things on my own. I would mark on the calendar the days I didn't binge or purge, I'd pray to be better, I'd do personal development, meditation, I would try to get up enough courage to tell someone, I would tell myself that next week would be better, and then I would lose control again. The cycle went on for over a year and a half before I decided that it was bigger than me. I needed to get help not only for me but also for my son.

Being a single mom with very little help was really overwhelming at times and having an eating disorder didn't make it easy to cope with the demands of life and being a mom. I didn't do much other than be a mom and work. I felt so alone, isolated and like a failure to my son. I would do anything for my son so it hurt so much knowing I couldn't get my eating disorder under control for him.

I stopped being social and fell into a bit of a depression, just going through the motions each day and not being fully present. For an overachiever, former athlete, gym rat and perfectionist it was really hard for me to admit that I couldn't gain control over my eating disorder. I desperately wanted to get my binging and purging under control for my son and my health.

When I was accepted into treatment, I was terrified. I feared that I wouldn't be able to get better, and that I would fail my son and have to accept that this was the way my life was going to be. It scared me to think that it might not work for me. The first day I was sitting at home making all the excuses in the world not to go to group. I was so worried that I couldn't even bring myself to go the first day. I got a call from the dietitian saying that there are others waiting and if I wasn't going to attend they needed to know so they could fill my spot. At that moment I made the commitment to myself and my son to stop making excuses. I didn't miss a day from that point forward and it was the best thing that I could have ever done.

I was given strategies to cope with my disorder and it helped me to better understand what was going on from a physical standpoint and that every food group has its place, even carbs. It took me a while to get my carbs in check; I just didn't believe that I really needed that many in my diet. It took me quite some time to get myself up to the minimum (of the Canada's Food Guide). I so did not enjoy tracking so one day the group leaders made me a deal with me. If

I could bring my carbs up to at least the minimum I wouldn't have to track anymore. Once I actually did it, it wasn't that scary. My meals were more balanced and satisfying which made me crave less and I felt full longer.

I have been recovered now for almost 6 months and I can honestly say, I wouldn't have been able to do it without Making Changes and Body Image (treatment groups). Everyone in the group made a scary and challenging situation a hell of a lot easier and the support from the team was amazing.

A HUGE breakthrough for me had to do with the scale. I used to step on the scale every morning and then multiple times throughout the day. So pretty much every morning the scale would determine what kind of day I was going to have, what I was going to wear, my mood, it was never good enough. What a horrible way to start the day! I haven't stepped on my scale for at least 3 months now and I have no desire to. It's not that I am scared to step on the scale, I just don't feel the need to anymore, and my weight has been steady for over 6 months, so really what's the point? I now allow my emotions and feelings to dictate the day I'm going to have, not a number on the scale.

I still find it hard at times and I can't say that it's always easy to stay on track and in control but I now have the skills and strategies to deal with the hard days. Plus my life has changed so much that there is no way I could bring myself to go back down that road again. I have worked so hard to get to where I am today and so each day I stay focused on what I am grateful for and the love that I feel in my heart for my son. I can honestly say that I am a better mom for it. I'm more present and patient, my relationships are more intentional and deeper, I'm less distracted, it's made me better at what I do, I'm more confident, more social, I feel like my old self again, I can go out with friends for dinner and focus on the conversation and not the food the whole time. I don't get hung up on what I'm eating and allow myself to have exceptional meals and treats! Carbs are my friend and the scale is NOT.

One thing that we all have to remember is that life is fragile and that we are all suffering in some way or another, but that doesn't mean that we can't get better. It's going to take time, hard work, dedication, consistency, self-love and compassion but if there is anything I know from the type of people WE are, we can do ANYTHING we put our minds to. You are here for a reason! You are brave and you are strong, you will overcome this hurdle and be free to live your life in peace and happiness.

An Artist's Perspective: A Note from Sharon

Although Katie did not have an image in mind, what struck me was her determination and her statement that "We can do anything we put our minds to." This reminded me of goals, and how goals can often propel us into action and set us on a course. Like the much quoted saying: Often when we aim for the moon, we end up in the stars.

Andrea: My Recovery Story

DIAGNOSIS: BINGE EATING DISORDER (WITH OCCASIONAL PURGING)

I have always had a very complex relationship with food. I've loved it and hated it all at the same time. I learned very early on that food was a great reward for a job well done, or would make me feel much better in times of sadness. After a while, food became my constant companion. I was eating when lonely, fearful, and sometimes for no reason at all. As my weight climbed and well-intentioned people gave me their unsolicited and sometimes brutally frank advice on how I should lose the weight, I began to eat in anger and yes sometimes just in spite.

My days were consumed with what I would eat, where I would get it from, and when I would eat it. I developed very clever ways to eat in private. I made hiding spots where I could keep my treats so others would not know about my binge, and most importantly so I would never have to share. My binge became more important to me than spending time with family or friends and as my weight ballooned, feeling ugly and fat, I made excuses for why I could not go out with them. Eventually, my weight made it too embarrassing to do activities I once loved.

Every now and then when I would grow disgusted with my appearance, I would do an extreme clean and remove all the offending food from my home. It was then that the deals with God began and the promise that if only he would help me lose weight, I would start tomorrow by moderately eating and making healthier food choices. Then when unable to cope with the pressures of the day and having no food in the house to console me, I would rummage through my baking cupboards to create a concoction that I am fairly certain the average person would have zero motivation to consume.

As many others with binge eating disorder do, I tried many diets. Some considered by health industry standards to be healthy and some downright bizarre. When all else failed and my weight began to tip the scales into the morbidly obese range, I developed the mistaken belief that if I purged I would either maintain or lose weight. At first I justified that purging was a necessary evil that would help me not gain weight, but over time I would come to realize how my desperation drove me to a behavior that could have life altering consequences for me.

During a binge I would shovel in as much food, as fast as I could in order to not to be discovered. In the moment of the binge, the food made me feel good, not only physically but emotionally. But then as that over-satiated feeling started to flood over me, the joy and comfort of the binge was replaced with regret, disgust and self-loathing. The fear of getting on the scale, something I did multiple times a day overwhelmed me.

One day, my son returned home from a day of high school. A young, bright, handsome boy having the time of his life. He had no worries, no cares or so I thought. I would learn he had secrets of his own. He was being teased at school about his weight. He began to express body image issues, ones that impacted his sense of self-esteem and self-worth. How did this happen? How did something that I believed only impacted me come to be my son's nemesis? It was then that I came to understand that my relationship with food was not just about me and my extra pounds. It was about something so much greater.

My entry into the eating disorders program wasn't easy. I believed that through this program they would teach me the secrets that would make me a thin and more socially attractive human being. I would become a role model for my son and correct my bad behavior. Imagine my shock to find out that I was likely leaving this program weighing generally the same weight as when I came in. What would be the point of that? I was however encouraged to stick it out and in doing so I would find what I came looking for.

So what did I find? I found that there were a number of genetic reasons why I was predetermined to be a voluptuous woman. I found that I, the daughter of immigrant parents, one with an eating disorder herself, who pushed their children to succeed and suppress emotions that were a hindrance to success, developed a core belief that would impact every relationship I would ever have. The belief that, "I was not enough."

I learned that it is ok to feel sadness, anger, loneliness, grief and joy. I can experience all my emotions in all their intensity and know that I can endure them, on my own, or with the support of family and friends. I no longer needed to suppress painful emotions with food. I learned that I am more than enough, for myself and for others. I am exactly the way I was meant to be. A beautiful, successful, witty, energetic and loving full figured gal who is loved by many just the way I am.

I have been asked if I consider myself cured. I would say I consider myself "enlightened". Does my core belief sometimes rear its ugly head and my companion food find its way into my life? Sure, it does. The only difference is that I am fully aware of it now and in being aware I can utilize the strategies I have been taught to forgive myself and immediately turn to my supports to deal with my emotions rather than my old friend food.

The world is a place full of different shapes, colors and tastes—as are the people in the world. Thank goodness for this diversity because a diverse world recognizes the value in all people.

Andrea: What I Wanted for My Pictures

I think imagery-wise I would like to see a voluptuous, confident and stylish woman with lots of shopping bags on my page. This is how I see myself. I've never enjoyed clothes and shopping as much as I have since I have accepted I am awesome just the way I am.

An Artist's Perspective: A Note from Sharon

I loved Andrea's request, as it reinforces how many women of all sizes and shapes love to shop. We all love to feel good about ourselves and to have the ability to make choices.

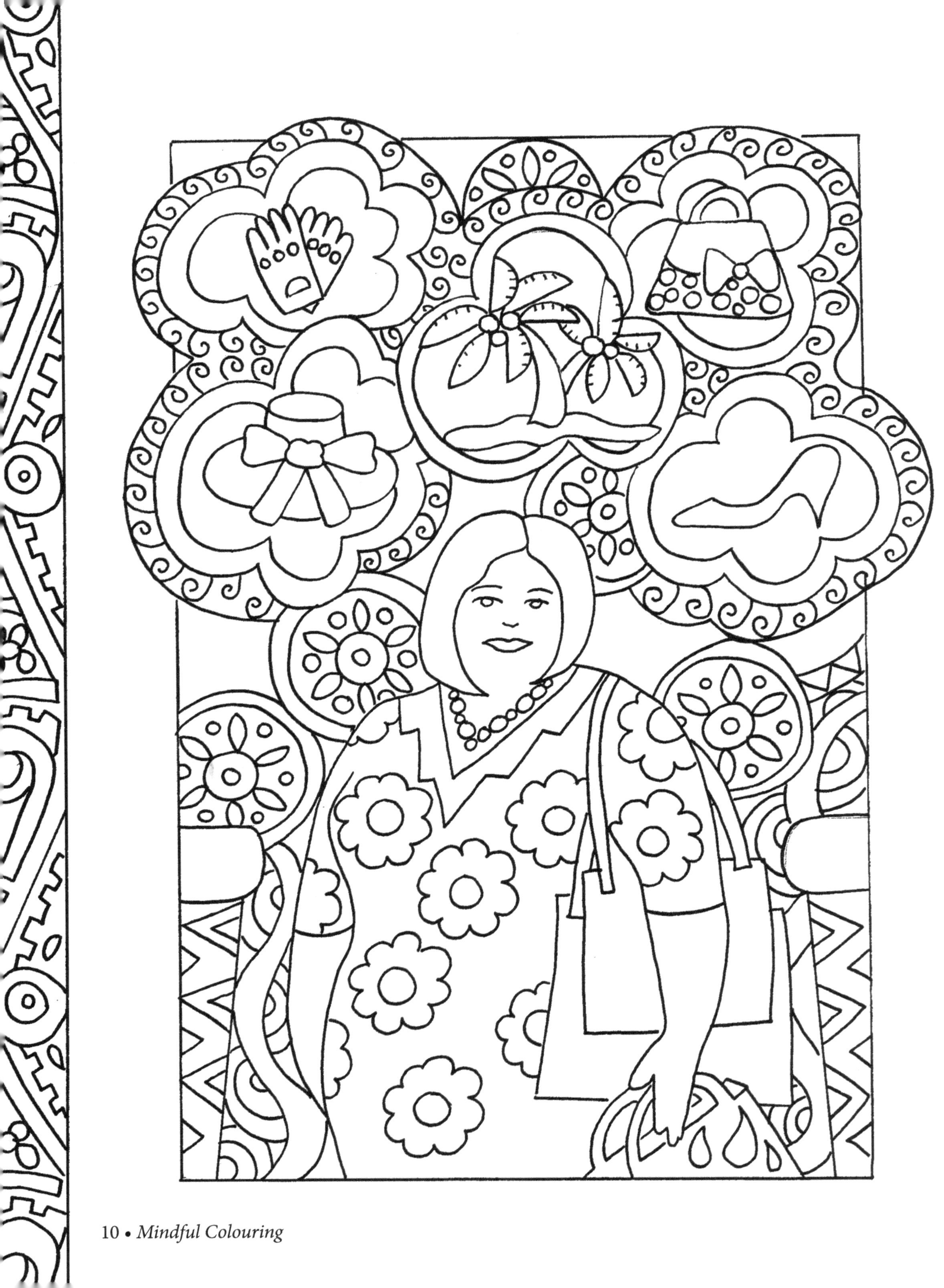

Recovery Theme 2

BEING OPEN TO NEW WAYS OF THINKING ABOUT THINGS

A Therapist's Perspective on Being Open to New Ways of Thinking about Things: Michèle

The majority of people who seek help for an eating disorder have already lived with that disorder for years; sometimes many years. If you are living with an eating disorder, you no doubt have developed strong beliefs about what you should be doing to have control over your weight and shape. You likely have rules about what and how much you should eat, and what you should not be eating. You also likely have strong opinions about what you should be doing in terms of exercise in order to manage your weight. As part of having an eating disorder, you will have devoted tremendous mental and emotional effort into trying to get this right. And despite these efforts, you may often feel like you are failing. Or, if you have been successful at controlling your weight, the "success" often feels precarious, or the cost to your life and well-being is so high that you spend much of your time preoccupied, anxious and unhappy. Many people who seek treatment describe being "tired" of living with their eating disorder. They hope that there is another, better way of living their lives and approaching weight and shape.

The trouble is that it can be so hard to change what you have believed for all these years. It can be very scary to go against the ideas you've lived by. In treatment, you are introduced to new information about weight, eating and physical activity. In the best of treatment, these ideas are based on good research from reliable sources. If you have doubts, be sure to ask questions so that you feel confident in the things you are learning. People in treatment often say they find the information they learn interesting, challenging and ultimately helpful. The most that could be asked is that you come to treatment open to considering new ways of thinking about things. As many of those seeking help have commented, what they have been doing isn't working. It makes sense to try something different!

A Patient's Perspective on Being Open to New Ways of Thinking about Things:
Marci

Being open to new ideas and different ways of thinking about things was key to my recovery. I knew that if I had all the answers I would have conquered this demon long ago. So I put aside my own preconceived notions about healthy eating, physical activity, weight loss, and good vs. bad foods…. I came to understand that by eating reasonable meals throughout the day combined with moderate physical activity that my body would find a natural set point. It took some time to get used to this idea especially after I spent most my life thinking I could control my weight— that if only I tried harder I could be thin.

Sara

Because of recovery, I am able to enjoy events and dinners with family and friends again (without constantly thinking about food and how I can "burn it off"). I can take time to find comfort in the little things—trying a new flavour of ice cream, feeling full after a holiday meal or sitting on the couch in my pyjamas all day while watching movies. There are many moments that I never thought I could appreciate until I have experienced recovery.

I won't deny that unhelpful thoughts still come through, but now I am able to react to those thoughts in a more effective way without acting on them.

Marci: My Recovery Story

DIAGNOSIS: BINGE EATING DISORDER

Like many girls I became concerned with my weight during puberty. I was tall for my age and developed early. I was a healthy weight but I weighed more than my friends. I remember my sister and my father teasing me as my body matured. I was disheartened. I started my first diet when I was thirteen.

Over time I turned to bingeing in response to excessive periods of restricting. I began regularly bingeing when I was 16. Just before my 16th birthday my father announced he was leaving my mother. I had a difficult relationship with my father. I tried very hard to please him but he was always distant. Despite my perfectionistic tendencies I never felt I was good enough—I never felt worthy of his love.

When my father left the home I felt I needed to protect my mother. She struggled to rebuild her life. My father had seemingly started over with little regard for the family he left behind and soon we became estranged. I binged and dieted all through high school and university.

I suffered from periods of depression and anxiety. During university my mother died. Shortly after, I ended an abusive relationship with a boyfriend. I felt very alone in the world. I turned to food for solace. I gained a lot of weight during this period. I was disgusted with my bingeing and weight gain. I started yet another diet.

I was a successful dieter and lost a lot of weight on a number of occasions. But after excessive restricting I would binge and after a few binges I gave up on dieting. I cycled back and forth between restricting and bingeing for 30 years. My weight yo-yoed as did my confidence. I tried nearly every diet. But in the end I gained more and more weight.

I used food to self–medicate, to soothe myself, to calm myself down, to deal with my anxiety and low moods. Initially during the binge I was euphoric but this shortly turned to loathing. I would consume thousands of calories in a just a few minutes and not stop until my stomach was bloated and painful. I was disgusted with myself. I was a well-educated successful woman and yet I was a prisoner to this behavior.

I had difficulty in relationships with men. I repeated unhealthy patterns over and over by selecting men who were distant. These relationships reinforced my belief that I was not loveable—that in some way I was flawed. These feelings fed my anxiety and depression and I binged to deal with the pain.

It was difficult to seek help because I was embarrassed. In my twenties binge eating had not even been recognized as a disorder. I could not find any treatment. I went on to binge 20 more years before finding help.

After a series of uncontrollable binges and accompanying weight gain I was emotionally exhausted. I knew the binge-diet cycle was not healthy for my physical body, but was equally as damaging for my soul. I had let the number on a scale determine my happiness, to control whether I enjoyed time with my friends, and whether I was worthy of respect and love in my relationships with men.

I sought out help once again. I found a treatment program for people with Binge Eating Disorder. I began to practice yoga regularly and reconnect with nature. In the past all my physical activity was designed to offset calories in an effort to lose weight. This time was different. I was practicing yoga and walking in the woods for pleasure, to relax, to connect to my soul. I knew I was on the right path.

Making changes in my relationship with food was particularly challenging. Being open to new ideas and different ways of thinking about things was key to my recovery. I knew that if I had all the answers I would have conquered this demon long ago. So I put aside my own preconceived notions about healthy eating, physical activity, weight loss, and good vs bad foods. It was difficult as I had spent 30 years of my life researching the latest diet, counting calories and carbohydrates, exercising for weight loss, and punishing myself for lack of control when I didn't follow the "plan".

I came to understand that by eating reasonable meals throughout the day combined with moderate physical activity that my body would find a natural set point. It took some time to get used to this idea especially after I spent most my life thinking I could control my weight—that if only I tried harder I could be thin.

I practiced the strategies I learned. It takes times to change the way you think of the world and yourself. I learned how my early childhood experiences had tainted my view of myself. I began to feel worthy of love and self-care.

I now eat balanced meals and snacks. I don't exclude food groups or restrict. I also eat for pleasure. I still have challenges with emotional eating. But I can identify it and I am able to address it before it leads to a binge. I do not let food or the scale control me. I eat birthday cake at birthdays, I don't hide my body behind baggie clothes, I no longer accept less than I deserve in my relationships with men, and I don't refer to myself in derogatory terms or berate my body.

I know recovery is a process and I have more work to do along the way. But my relationship with food and my body has changed. I practice yoga regularly and hike the trails connecting with nature and myself. I am grateful for my body and all that it does for me. This is the first time in 30 years that I did not make a new year's resolution to lose weight. But a weight has been lifted. I am truly happy and I am shining from within.

An Artist's Perspective: A Note From Sharon

Marci mentioned how yoga and walks in nature connected her to her soul. I completely understood. I chose to create a person doing yoga, coming out of a lotus flower. Being a student of yoga, it was not surprising that her other image was a mandala.

Sara: My Recovery Story

DIAGNOSIS: ANOREXIA NERVOSA, RESTRICTING TYPE

I try to write this without being a perfectionist or worrying that I am saying the right things. There is no 'right' or 'wrong' way to recover. One of the most challenging aspects about recovery is accepting that it is not a linear process. I had an expectation that recovery would just progress until I was at a 'normal' weight and that I would feel better than I ever had. Recovery doesn't work like that. The road to recovery is one that is difficult and full of speed bumps. Finding my set point and then tolerating my body and accepting the change has been, and will continue to be, challenging. I was told that body image concerns would be a tough obstacle to overcome in the later stages of recovery and that is true for me. Identifying my core beliefs and the real reason for my distress about my weight and shape is a very important aspect of recovery. I still struggle with this and there are days when the ED threatens my vulnerabilities. The difference now is that I have found the strength to push back. Throughout recovery, I have discovered so much about myself and I have gained insight into the nature of the disease.

I never imagined my life would turn out this way. Having an eating disorder and then undergoing a demanding course of recovery is not what I had expected. However, it has been through this process of recovery that I have developed a new-found confidence. I reflect on the fact that I made it through a Day Hospital Program for three months, in another city, with strangers, at my weakest point. Life is full of challenging situations and I am now confident that I have the perseverance and strength to get through them.

History of my eating disorder:

I never really considered myself a perfectionist. I tried really hard in school and often worried a little too much about things (e.g., what people thought about me, getting a bad grade, looking/sounding 'dumb'). The worry and fear prevented me from being social and from stepping out of my comfort zone. My personality is a mix of being shy, introverted, emotional and sensitive, which I believe are qualities that can be both advantageous and detrimental.

At the end of high school and throughout university, I slowly became obsessed with appearance and with a desire to be thin and attractive. This obsession compelled me to exercise more and change my diet. In my final year of university, I felt very unsure and worried of my future. I didn't have a goal for after graduation. Over time, I became consumed with thoughts of weight gain and body shape—I was never satisfied with myself.

It took over a year to realize I even had a problem. I knew I was underweight but the ED had overcome all of my thoughts. Exercise was a form of numbing myself. I didn't want to push myself to those limits but I felt I had no choice. The ED only gave me one choice: do more, push my limit, eat less and exercise more than last time. Because if I didn't do more, then I had failed; and anything else I did was a waste. It wasn't about being thin or looking good anymore. I knew I looked ill. I knew what I was doing was not good for me and that it was causing my heart rate to plummet. But it didn't stop me. I was trapped in a cycle of wake up, work out and restrict, go to bed scared and upset about what I was doing, promising myself that things would change and that I would eat more and exercise less. But, I was just fooling myself. Nothing changed. If I wasn't able to exercise, I compensated by eating less. If I ate more food than I thought was 'acceptable', I exercised harder and longer. I was constantly battling my thoughts and no matter what, I lost. I was losing myself to the ED. I was no longer the same person.

My motivation for recovery was wanting to feel something different—something better than I was feeling during my illness. I wanted to become better than I ever was. A new person. Although (I know now) I set unrealistic expectations for what recovery should look like, I used those expectations as a stepping stone towards recovery.

I was/ am lucky to have such a great support system. I wouldn't be writing this story if it weren't for them. The ED can bring you to a sad and dark place. I was in this darkness for a while and I brought the gloom with me wherever I went. It clouded over my relationships and hid the joy that I used to have when I was with these people. I can't thank my family and boyfriend enough for pulling me from the darkness and showing me that path to recovery. No matter how much I wanted to isolate myself from the world, they remained by my side. They knew recovery was possible long before I did. The advice I give to those in any stage of their illness or recovery is to reach out and use your support system. Don't go through this alone. Whether it is family, friends, doctors, or others who are struggling with this as well, find comfort in knowing that there are people who can help you move forward in recovery.

It has taken me a long time to find who I really am as a person. I still don't think I have found it. If there is one thing this disorder has taught me, it is the ability to look deep within myself to figure out how I have gotten to this point in recovery, to this point in my life. I may not have all of the answers (although I wish I did), but at least I can say I am a little bit stronger than I was. I am more aware of my feelings and I am better able to recognize where my emotions are coming from. I find value in being able to self-reflect. I value the insight I have gained through this whole experience. I may not be fully recovered or 100% in tune with my emotions and thoughts. But I am confident in my ability to try to be the best me, not only for myself, but also for my family and my friends.

Sara: What I Wanted for My Pictures

I think I'd like to incorporate a symbol or representation of serenity. I really like the saying, "Serenity comes when you trade expectations for acceptance." I chose this because I've been told that I come across as serene and calm. I've found this surprising because on the inside I was constantly battling my fears and worries. This concept of being in a state of peacefulness and tranquility stuck with me and gave me the strength in knowing that it is achievable if I just let go of my expectations.

An Artist's Perspective: A Note from Sharon

Serenity. For Sara, immediately images for being present in the moment came to mind. What better way to find serenity than to appreciate the beauty that surrounds us—like a willow tree, or a rock sculpture to help one achieve a state of peacefulness.

Recovery Theme 3

BEING WILLING TO TRUST IN THE HELP YOU RECEIVE

A Therapist's Perspective on Being Willing to Trust in the Help You Receive: Michèle

I have often thought that recovery from an eating disorder is particularly challenging in our culture. Ideally, a person wanting to recover could look at people around them for good examples of what "healthy" means. Instead, there are wildly different and conflicting opinions about what constitutes healthy eating, healthy activity and good body image—and no shortage of people willing to give you their opinions. As a person recovering, it can be hard to know who to trust and what to believe.

If you are coming for treatment, it is useful to think of it as a time during which you are participating in an experiment. You can't know for sure that you will feel better at the end of treatment. However, you can't know whether the experiment of recovery has worked for you unless you give it a truly genuine effort. People who recover often say that they made the choice to trust in the help they received; this is the experiment. Commit to a time frame in which you will fully participate in the experiment of recovery, and when things get hard, remind yourself that this is an experiment you have promised yourself to complete. Once you have worked at overcoming your symptoms and improving body image, you will be in the best position to decide if the experiment has worked. At that point, the choice of whether to continue with recovery will be entirely yours.

A Patient's Perspective on
Being Willing to Trust in the Help You Receive:
Andrea

Being willing to trust was not something that came naturally to me. I wanted to be in control, and trusting in the help I was receiving felt like I was giving up control. During the process of recovery I continually reminded myself that the individuals providing help were professionals and wanted the best for me. Being willing to trust in the help I was receiving allowed me to fully embrace the therapy and recovery process. Through welcoming, accepting, and trusting help, I learned to trust myself and my body, and believe that recovery is possible.

Kristen

For me and my recovery, trust in the program was an element of paramount importance. I put 100% of my trust in my team. I believed what they told me to be true and that they weren't lying to me. It was a choice I made to believe them and though at times I followed blindly, I always did so with total faith that they were leading me in the absolute right direction. By trusting others to help me, I was able to learn to help myself and I eventually learned that I can trust myself as well.

Andrea: My Recovery Story

DIAGNOSIS: ANOREXIA NERVOSA, RESTRICTING TYPE

I grew up in a loving household with my parents and older brother. With a strong Ukrainian influence in my life, food was a form of love and I participated in many cultural activities. I took piano and dance lessons and enjoyed travelling and family activities. I was a social butterfly and a happy individual. My body reached puberty when I was 10 years old and I found myself chubby compared to my peers. I was teased about my weight and shape so I went online to look for healthy lifestyle tips. I started paying attention to food groups and portion sizes and began exercising on a regular basis. I felt good about my behaviours and my family members complimented my willpower and interest in health at such a young age.

Over the next two years my portion sizes gradually got smaller, I became very strict about the foods I would and would not eat, and I exercised for hours every day. I stopped going out to restaurants, started bringing my own food to family functions, and ate at the same time every day. Before I knew it, I was completely preoccupied with food and activity and was undereating and over-exercising. In addition to being preoccupied with my weight and food intake, I also became judgmental of my family's weight and food intake. I criticized what my family members ate and lectured them for not being more active. Physically, I lost weight and developed amenorrhea [loss of menstrual period]. Socially, I was isolated and lost many of my friends. Emotionally, I was unhappy and lost all interest in hobbies. Somehow my life became a world of strict rules, and rather than feeling in control of my life, I felt like all the rules were controlling me. While I continued with my day to day existence, I had this feeling that something was not right and eventually approached my parents and told them I needed help.

My parents were very supportive and it took me a few tries to find the help I needed. Finding a therapist I connected with and felt comfortable with was trial and error. I was diagnosed with anorexia nervosa and found myself in weekly outpatient individual therapy. Throughout my many years in therapy, I learned a tremendous amount about myself and the nature of my eating disorder. The words "perfectionist", "purist", "rigid", "routine", "depression", and "anxiety" were regularly used to describe my experience. I spent years trying to understand and break the rules of my eating disorder. The rigidity of the rules interfered in so many aspects of my life. The slightest change to my schedule or routine would throw me into a spiral of anxiety. The anxiety I experienced was extremely difficult to overcome. My therapist suggested medication to help lessen the stress, and after resisting the idea for a while, I agreed to try medication. This was one of the best decisions I made. The combination of therapy and medication made my anxiety and emotions less traumatic and more manageable.

For several years I worked with my therapist to develop coping skills and increase my food intake and variety. Developing coping skills was easy compared to restoring my weight. For years I was weighed weekly, and for many weeks my weight stayed the same. When my weight did not change, my therapist and I worked together to increase my daily intake and/or assess my exercise to see where it could be modified. At first I lied about eating additional food or changing my exercise. There was still a part of me that found comfort in the familiarity of my eating disorder. I wanted to feel in control and I was extremely afraid of change. Being honest with my therapist and myself was very difficult, however it helped me realize that every week I did not change my behaviour was another week of cheating myself and my recovery progress.

Despite frustrations and anxiety about gaining weight, I trusted my therapist, slowly accepted the process, and increased my food intake. I eventually stopped exercising and was eating so much food on a regular basis that my jaw would sometimes hurt from chewing. In order for me to feel safe and less anxious, my eating was very mechanical for many years. Due to my low weight and slow weight restoration, I had amenorrhea for about six years. I went for regular bone density tests during my recovery and was diagnosed with osteoporosis when I was 19 years old. It was scary to know that my bones were similar to those of a 70 year old woman. Until this point my body seemed invincible no matter how poorly it was treated. Being told I have osteoporosis was the wake-up call I needed to speed up my recovery. As I continued to gain weight and eat new foods, I ended up overshooting my natural weight. I began menstruating again, and when I was 21 years old my bone density was back in the normal range. I remained at a higher weight for a while, and eventually my appetite naturally changed and my weight settled at a healthy place.

Working through my eating disorder and actively working towards recovery was exhausting at times. I left some therapy sessions feeling energized and enthusiastic and left others feeling completely defeated. Overcoming all of the irrational and illogical rules of my eating disorder was extremely challenging and extremely rewarding. I did this through therapy sessions to develop my confidence and coping skills and through regular exposures. Exposures included eating treats and desserts, eating with others, eating at different times, going to restaurants, and being more flexible with physical activity. My therapist always reminded me that I always lived to tell the tale and that everything would be okay. As I continued to expose myself and kept trying new and unfamiliar things, it got easier and I cried a little less each time. Eventually I reached a place where I began suggesting exposures and trying new things, and actually found enjoyment in the process.

I have been in recovery for about five years. I consider myself fully in recovery but I am hesitant to say that I am fully recovered. For me, saying "fully recovered" implies that it is past tense, and the last time I said I was fully recovered I ended up relapsing. When I attended therapy between the ages of 13 and 19, I viewed recovery as a destination and something I would achieve and be done with. With this perspective I got lazy and let my defenses down. I relapsed at the age of 23 and went back to therapy for another two years and participated in a body image group. While I will always consider recovery a tremendous achievement, I now view it as a process and active phase of life. With the knowledge, awareness, and coping skills I gained and developed in therapy, being in recovery and living each day in wellness has become second nature.

My experience with an eating disorder has shaped the person I am today. In hindsight, I am grateful for my eating disorder experience and the incredible ways it challenged me and allowed me to grow. The years of therapy and internal reflection have enabled me to be very mindful and compassionate, to myself and others. Recovery has helped me to appreciate my uniqueness and developed a healthy and happy relationship with food, activity, and my body. In recovery I feel physically and mentally strong, flexible, confident, capable, authentic, and joyful. I am a social butterfly again. During my time in therapy I learned about my temperament—how I am naturally a perfectionist who prefers structure and routine. These traits allow me to be a very successful individual, and they also make me vulnerable to an eating disorder. In recovery I continue to embrace my temperament, monitor my natural tendencies, and work on the parts of my personality that do not come easily to me such as being messy and going with the flow.

Andrea: What I Wanted for My Pictures

I would like Sharon to include the following in the picture associated with my section: 1) A sea turtle—symbolizing perseverance, endurance, longevity, and the slow and steady process of recovery; and 2) A butterfly—symbolizing re-discovering myself as a social butterfly and the transformation that occurs during recovery.

An Artist's Perspective: A Note from Sharon

Wonderful that Andrea wanted both the sea turtle and the butterfly for her pictures. As she noted, they symbolize the process of recovery and have special meaning for her.

Kristen: My Recovery Story

DIAGNOSIS: BULIMIA NERVOSA

Today, on a physical level, I now consider myself recovered from the eating disorder. On an emotional and spiritual level, however, I consider myself to be in a perpetual state of joyful recovering, meaning that I am now on a progressive path of regaining possession of the knowledge of self, of who I am as a person.

My "physical" eating disorder began when I was 18 but the emotional disconnection I had with myself which I believe was the propagating environment for the eating disorder began much earlier. The eating disorder soil had been unwittingly fertilized and so its life inevitably began. Mostly, my eating disorder could be characterized as bulimia, and fettered with periods of food restriction, but really it was a profoundly strong, yet most fundamentally misaligned, call for love and acceptance. Love, I had learned early on, was conditional and I cleverly observed that my behaviour could alter conditions so that people would "love" me. Though it (the ED) never did harvest enough love to fill the empty hole in my heart, it served well enough that I clung fiercely to it for about 22 years, not knowing any other way. I was at the end of my proverbial rope when I finally committed myself to treatment, and my life to recovering. The hole was beyond empty and all attempts I had made to fill it, even with the eating disorder behaviour, were no longer working. Logically, I truly felt that death was the next step in the natural progression of things, unless I wanted to try a different path. I was at a fork in the road and terribly frightened. I could choose death (the way of which I knew) or I could choose life (the way of which I had no clue). I chose life.

I was overly optimistic when I began treatment but my enthusiasm was short-lived. I encountered obstacles I didn't even know were in the way. I felt blindsided and completely overwhelmed. I quickly learned that recovery was going to show me lots of things about myself that I'd spent all of my life avoiding. It was tremendously painful. I struggled with the discomfort of a changing body. I struggled with depression and anxiety. I struggled with shame. I struggled with finding any sense of assurance that I was doing it right. And I really struggled with losing control of a world which, in truth, I actually had zero control over. I mean, my whole sense of self-worth was wrapped up in the eating disorder and I was being asked to let it go. That was the hardest part of recovery for me, letting go. Letting go of a very specific self I'd spent well over 22 years creating and letting go of the idea that there was a right way to recover, a right way to be healthy, a right way to be me. I had to learn to let go of everything I thought I knew—about life, about, myself, about recovering. I had to let go of the outcome and trust that the process of becoming me and becoming well would take care of itself. And remarkably, I learned that this was true. It did take care of itself in very wonderful and miraculous ways.

Recovery for me has opened a space inside of me through which life experience can now pass with gentle observation. Recovery exposed the flame of worthiness in me that I didn't think I'd ever find. Each day now is a tender experiment in finding what stokes that flame as well as learning what smothers it, and then willfully choosing which to do with loving kindness.

Kristen: What I Wanted for My Pictures

My whole recovery has been about finding **me**—rooting and grounding. I have a very fond appreciation of very large, very old trees—their roots and history run deep and they are incredibly steadfast and strong. They are a beautiful representation of human will and determination.

An Artist's Perspective: A Note from Sharon

I never tire of drawing trees, and agree with Kristen that trees are symbols of rooting and grounding. And yes, they definitely represent our connection with the earth, and our ability to be flexible, sturdy and weather the storm.

Recovery Theme 4

DOING THINGS THAT SCARE YOU

A Therapist's Perspective on Doing Things That Scare You: Michèle

People who recover from an eating disorder often describe it as the hardest thing they have ever done; and in the end, the most rewarding. Recovery is hard because it requires you to tolerate feeling anxious, uncomfortable or guilty. The scary things you must face in recovery make for quite a long list: eating foods you feel are "bad"; tolerating feeling full when you are afraid it will make you fat(ter); not purging when you know it will give you relief; cutting back your activity even when it leaves you feeling "lazy"; sitting with emotions when you know that binge eating would allow you to escape; tolerating change to your body; tolerating your body remaining the same; and going out to face the world with an imperfect body when you so fear other people's judgments. With all these fears, how is it that recovery would ever feel rewarding?

I often tell the people I see in treatment that you have to be willing to be afraid to find out that you are safe. To live with an eating disorder is to be ruled by fear all the time – fears related to eating and activity, fears related to weight, and fears related to what others think of you. You can only make these fears smaller if you face them. Facing fears is always easier when you have planned and prepared for your "exposure" to the thing you fear. To make fears go away, you need to face that fear over and over, or for long enough, that you no longer feel afraid. And since none of us *like* feeling afraid, you are more likely to face your fears when you have a therapist to whom you can be accountable. The immense feeling of freedom that results from no longer feeling afraid is the reward of recovery. In this freedom comes the opportunity to find joy in so many aspects of life. There is joy in small things like being able to share in a meal; and joy in larger things like feeling confident in your body. Discovering that you can face things that make you afraid or uncomfortable gives you control over your life. Doing things that scare you is the way out of the prison of the eating disorder.

A Patient's Perspective on
Doing Things That Scare You:
Stephanie

Doing things that scare you …

I feel like this topic is very fitting for me, because it is basically how I ended up in recovery from my eating disorder. I believe that you have to jump all in, even when it's *terrifying*; not just when it's scary. I was told early in recovery that the more you push yourself to jump all in, the greater benefit there will be. So I jumped in, and then was like "What the HELL am I doing?" It turns out that it was the best way to learn—I made it through the week! I started eating grains; I challenged negative thoughts; and put up some great boundaries all within a very short amount of time. Looking back, I wouldn't have done it any other way, but at the time did not know if I would make it. If you're feeling the same way, you will make it. I promise.

Stephanie: My Recovery Story

DIAGNOSIS: ANOREXIA NERVOSA, BINGE EATING/PURGING TYPE

When embarking on recovery, the most important thing to know is to start now, in the middle of a mess. There is no waiting until tomorrow; do the best you can with today. If you can take baby steps, take them. If you can take giant leaps, take them. Whatever it is, just keep moving in the direction you want to go but remember to have compassion on the days you slip back. The slips do not define you; they remind you what you've committed to and why it is so important. Before reading on, I want you to know that I'm doing well. Although my story includes trauma, it also includes a beautiful journey of healing and self-discovery. I have been in recovery for just under a year. Although, I've made great progress, I do not consider myself recovered as I feel that recovery is an on-going process.

I am told that I never give myself enough credit. I'm always moving from one thing to the next, never acknowledging the accomplishments in the middle. This isn't just an adult thing. I've never done it, but I'd like to acknowledge that the superhero who deserves the most credit is the child-sized me, because without her kind of superhero strength, determination and resilience, I wouldn't be here. I'd be dead.

As a child, I made it through the toughest series of events that, in my mind, I will ever have to go through—but sometimes I find myself still living in this space where those events are seeded so deeply within my thoughts and beliefs that changing them feels like the most impossible task. Break-ups pale in comparison to the pain associated with making it through a childhood filled with sexual abuse and then living in the aftermath.

My abuse started when I was around 6 and went on until about the age of 12 or 13. I've blocked out so much, I can barely even remember. Those horrible six years have impacted the last three decades of my life. Assuming I live until I'm 90 (fingers crossed), a third of my life has been filled with controlling emotions, binge-eating, restricting and rock-bottom days just trying to navigate my way to a place where I felt like I could make my own choices and no longer need to protect myself or control my world with food.

Growing up, I was told I was so confident, beautiful and intelligent—but why would I believe anything when my childhood was based mostly around learning how to lie and accept being lied to by people that were supposed to protect me? The lines began to blur between my worth as a person and my worth as a body. This is when the eating disorder began.

As a child I had less ability to protect myself, so I found protection and comfort in food. It was a coping mechanism for dealing with the emotions I was too young to navigate. As I got older the eating disorder evolved into restriction instead of only bingeing but eventually all of the restriction caught up to me and I started bingeing again. In order to compensate for the bingeing, I began exercising, a lot. This helped me maintain a reasonable weight range for a while and allowed me to fly under the radar, or so I thought. However, I learned the hard way that my body could not sustain this punishment, nor did it deserve it. I tore my knee, suffered bladder incontinence, amenorrhea and terrible mood swings. As a result, I had to take over a year off of exercise completely. It was a difficult year, but really put my life in perspective. I needed to recover.

Recovery was hard. I cried, a lot. My husband had to drop me off at the door of St. Joe's on

more than one occasion because I did not want to go to group. I bartered for "less grains" and was the most skeptical person in the room. But I committed to the experiment of recovery on the first day of group, and I am still committed to this day.

For me, one of the most difficult parts of recovery was distancing myself from my parents and my family but I needed to do what was best for me and for my health. It wasn't forever; we have started to mend parts of our relationship, but it is different. The relationship is on my terms and no longer sends me into a tailspin of emotion and cookies.

Weight restoration was also a big challenge, especially being around friends and athletes who are doing everything the opposite of what I am doing. I got through it by reminding myself that what I'm doing is for me, not for them. If they want to reach a race weight, or run every day, they can—but I do not have to be a part of it because I have committed myself to recovery, compassion and self-love.

I never thought there would be a day that I would look in the mirror and say "You're one beautiful chick!" But now I can. Not because of the way my body looks but because I can look myself in the eye without feeling ashamed of what I see. I'm so proud of myself for not only getting to this day, but for this day to be happening more and more.

Recovery has been the best thing that has ever happened to me. The biggest impact has been on my emotions. I am no longer raging on the edge of a nervous breakdown from never eating a carb. I'm stable and grounded. I feel good. I can pay attention in conversations at restaurants. I can eat with freedom and I feel way more comfortable in my own skin, even with the weight restoration.

Stephanie: What I Wanted for My Pictures

A map with checkpoints or flags—recovery is a process with valleys and mountains or highs and lows. Someone jumping off a waterfall.

An Artist's Perspective: A Note from Sharon

How true it is that recovery is a circuitous journey, with many valleys and hills, so this is what her one picture captures. Secondly, having a person jumping over a waterfall, experiencing fear, risk taking and freedom is so much like the recovery journey with an eating disorder.

Recovery Theme 5

BEING WILLING TO RELY ON THE STRUCTURE OF THERAPY WHILE TOLERATING CHANGE

A Therapist's Perspective on Being Willing to Rely on the Structure of Therapy While Tolerating Change: Michèle

If you want to recover from your eating disorder, this likely means that you have some willingness to change and to try something new. You may have already tried to make changes on your own, before coming to therapy. Unfortunately, when you are trying to make changes on your own, it is very difficult to know what changes are the *right* changes. Without confidence, the changes people make tend to be small and tentative. And it is so easy to fall back into old ways when you are anxious and unsure of what you are doing.

People who recover often say that they found it helpful to rely on the structure of therapy while they were facing the anxiety of change. Good therapy will provide education to help lay out the path in front of you. We all do better facing things we fear when we know what is in front of us and have a chance to prepare. As part of therapy, you will be asked to plan ahead. With planning, you are more likely to be able to do something scary (like add something new to what you are eating), than if you leave decisions to the last minute. At the last minute, having to decide *when* you are going to eat and *what* you are going to eat on top of *if* you are going to eat, can be enough to make change impossible. Planning keeps the decision simple—are you going to do what you planned to do? As part of therapy, you will also be asked to track your eating and activity. Without this self-monitoring, it is easy to fool, or frighten yourself about the amount of food you are eating or activity you are doing. You will also be asked to track your thoughts, feelings and circumstances. Without this information, it is hard to challenge your fears or problem-solve to prevent future symptoms. I will acknowledge that the structure of therapy—the planning and the tracking and the problem-solving—can seem like tedious work. And … it is also your best support in working through changes that we know are going to make you anxious. To have the best chance of recovery, decide you will fully commit to the work in front of you.

A Patient's Perspective on Being Willing to
Rely on the Structure of Therapy While Tolerating Change:
Cheryl

As you embark on your journey to overcome BED, have faith in the process. Change takes time, knowledge, and courage, and at times, it may feel like you are in a state of chaos. Many of the recommendations will seem foreign at first, and may challenge your core beliefs. The methodology works if you have the perseverance to stay the course. Trust in the experts who will provide you with the knowledge, guidance and support to succeed, they are key to your recovery.

Stephanie

Relying on the structure of therapy was crucial in my recovery. I think that if I wasn't being monitored through my therapy I would have viewed my eating habits and weight change as another failure. Having guidance and support reassured me that change was OK and because of that I was OK with it.

Cheryl: My Recovery Story

DIAGNOSIS: BINGE EATING DISORDER

At 5'7" and a size 10, I wasn't the typical persona of a binge eater. My actions and inner struggle however, would indicate that I embodied the characteristics of a person with BED, binge eating disorder. For many years I battled this disease in secret, thinking I am smart and strong, and I should be able to overcome this affliction on my own. It was hard to admit to myself that I had a problem, let alone to those around me, so I suffered in silence. After many failed attempts, I decided to seek medical attention. I encountered a lack of understanding and disappointing results with various professionals, that is, until I discovered St. Joseph's Eating Disorders Clinic.

In my discussions with the psychologist, I came to understand that BED held physiological and psychological components. Getting on a normalized eating plan was key and there were beliefs I had to challenge in order to get there. One of the first ideas I confronted was my resistance to carbohydrates. It became apparent that the food group I was avoiding led to my binges mid-afternoon. The pantry had become my place of refuge. Adding fiber to my breakfast not only helped my digestion, but more importantly, combatted my afternoon cravings and submission to everything and anything that looked even slightly appealing.

My perfectionist tendencies had been addressed in other areas of my life; however, they still reared their ugly head in my beliefs about food and eating. I was extremely black and white when it came to treats and would deprive myself of everything not on my own personal 'approved' list. This rigid mindset did not apply to bingeing. I refused samples at the grocery store, wouldn't have dessert, and refused to incorporate my perceived 'bad' foods into my daily eating. Deprivation was a huge obstacle to overcome. I made a list of foods I avoided and I was told to incorporate them into everyday life. "But I will get fat if I eat these," I protested. "You will get fat if you DON'T eat them," was the reply. It was an incredibly profound statement for me. I finally understood that my long rooted belief in deprivation and perfectionism contributed to my bingeing.

Body image was another area that needed to be addressed. I learned that how I felt about my body had nothing to do with my actual size. One of the most impactful exercises was to write a letter from my thighs to myself. Written from the voice of my beaten up thighs, I conveyed their distress regarding the harsh judgment I had inflicted upon them. They asked, instead, that I celebrate all that they do for me to enjoy life. The response from me to my thighs was a heartfelt apology for so many years of unkind criticism. I shed many tears writing these letters and over time I truly came to embrace my thighs and focus on their functionality. I would highly recommend you complete this exercise during your recovery as it had an incredible impact on how I look at and feel about my body.

As I approach the first year anniversary, I consider myself a recovered binge eater who still faces the occasional challenge. Revisiting my normalized eating plan and some gentle introspection helps gets me back on track. I have been freed; released from the beliefs that kept me bound in self-destructive behavior. I no longer carry the burden of this disease that plagued me for so many years, of which I suffered alone. I have overcome one of my biggest challenges. I have my life back.

An Artist's Perspective: A Note from Sharon

For Cheryl I created two pictures of dolphins. When I see dolphins, I imagine their freedom as they probe the depths of the sea. And what a wonderful symbol for Cheryl who can now see herself as free from a long-time, deep-seated behaviour.

Stephanie: My Recovery Story

DIAGNOSIS: OTHER SPECIFIED FEEDING AND EATING DISORDERS, PURGING DISORDER WITH SUBJECTIVE BINGES

Being Me!

I was 23 and getting married to the man of my dreams. Dress shopping was the most exciting part of what was to be my fairytale day. As I picked out dresses to try on, not one of their sample sizes fit me. I was told I would need to buy a "plus" size dress. I was devastated. How could I be "plus" sized, a size 14? The good news was that I had a year to lose weight. About six months before my wedding, I became desperate to lose weight, and for some reason I experimented with bulimic behavior. I started purging after every meal. I lost about three dress sizes in four months and my dress had to be drastically altered. I was so happy. People complimented me on my weight loss and how fabulous I looked. I LOVED having all of this positive attention, which I so desperately craved.

The wedding came and went, I continued to purge and I began to gain weight and lose weight. I got pregnant with twins; I gained weight and lost weight. I started exercising; I lost weight and gained it again. The cycle was vicious, and my eating disorder continued to be a huge facet of my life. I promised many times I would stop but somehow binging kept creeping up in my life, especially as a way to cope with unwanted feelings.

Fast forward 12 years. After a devastating fight with my family, I decided I needed to seek help for my eating disorder. I realized that I couldn't stop this on my own and my mental health was suffering. Although I wanted help, I didn't believe I was worthy of getting help for this "problem" because it wasn't serious enough. Why? Well I wasn't thin, I had no real physical health problems and honestly I didn't believe I had a true eating disorder. I didn't really admit it to myself. I was told that I was being selfish, self-absorbed, only thinking of myself. In reality I was thinking about what others were thinking of me. I was never truly thinking of myself, at least not in a positive way.

I finally sought help through my family doctor and to my surprise she actually cared. She was very concerned for my health, physically and mentally. I finally felt that maybe I was worth it somehow. My doctor found an eating disorder outpatient clinic for me, but the waiting list was at least two to three months. That was a long wait for me especially given how hard it was for me to ask for help, so I really wanted help now. I luckily was able to find my angel, the psychologist I worked with. At first we worked on my mental health issues with my family. I had a lot of them. I was diagnosed with generalized anxiety disorder, mood disorder, and OCD. I was shocked to learn that the deep and intense feelings I've had my whole life hadn't been made up; rather, I was actually not equipped or taught how to deal with my emotions. On top of this I needed to deal with my bulimia. Yes, I was bulimic. I actually never said that out loud. I was scared what others would say or think about me. But I needed to admit it to myself. My psychologist and I worked on an eating plan each week. We tracked my purge episodes to help figure out why I purged to plan a way to avert such urges in the future. It was hard to eat all I was supposed to eat. I ate "scary" foods, like pizza, pasta, and chocolate, all without purging.

After about four months of seeing my psychologist on a weekly basis, we decided I was well enough to enroll me in a body image group. I was scared because I've never spoken with anyone besides my immediate family and my psychologist about my eating disorder and now I was going to talk with strangers about it and the struggles I have with my body. There were three other beautiful women in my group and after the first few weeks I felt comfortable with them. We were challenged with many exercises, and you know what I discovered? That I was okay the way I was. I began to realize that I was a good person and that people liked me for me, not because of how thin or big I was. I realized that I hadn't felt comfortable with who I was my whole life until now. I was trying to be something that wasn't me.

Life is hard and we are constantly told who we should be and what we should look like, and I got lost in that. All I really wanted to be was a kind person. And that is how I live my life in the present. I treat people with respect, love, and compassion, because that's what really matters in life. I've learned that what others think of me doesn't matter if I don't allow it to matter.

I've been through many ups and downs, especially with depression, since I've been through my recovery. When my mood is low, I can have difficulty with purging again. When and if I purge, I don't look at it as a failure; rather, I remind myself of all I have accomplished to get to where I am today and move on to tomorrow. Will I ever be purge free? I don't know, but I do hope one day I can say that I am. Right now I live each day to its fullest and thank my body for doing all it does for me because the old me would have listened to her ED and believed that she wasn't worthy. I AM WORTHY and I can finally BE ME!

Stephanie: What I Wanted for My Pictures

When I think of recovery I imagine being free. I imagine flying away from all that brought me down. The image of my tattoo would be cool to incorporate in the page. It has the eating disorder symbol, mental health symbol, birds flying off (me and my hubby) and the feathers (I call them) represent all those who helped me through my recovery.

An Artist's Perspective: A Note from Sharon

Stephanie's images completely revolved around her recovery tattoo, as it was extremely important to her and what it represented. I included her tattoo in the two images, to represent freedom in the form of flight.

Recovery Theme 6

FINDING HEALTHY WAYS TO TOLERATE DIFFICULT EMOTIONS

A Therapist's Perspective on Finding Healthy Ways to Tolerate Difficult Emotions: Michèle

There are many ways in which emotions can play a part in an eating disorder. When you still have your eating disorder, life's emotions can make it difficult for you to keep restricting your food or being "good". In these cases, emotions lead to a cascade of symptoms such as binge eating and/or purging. Sometimes symptoms such as binge eating, restricting, over-exercising or purging can be used *deliberately*, because they help you move away from difficult emotions; emotions like sadness, anxiety, loneliness or anger. And almost all the time, the eating disorder can leave you feeling that your self-worth is directly related to your weight. The scale, the mirror or your clothes can send you soaring to an emotional high, or plummeting to the depths of despair and self-hatred. Because managing your weight seems so important, the symptoms of your eating disorder may feel like the only way you have to protect your self-worth, and feel safe or in control.

The challenge of recovery is to find healthier ways to tolerate difficult emotions and to feel good about yourself. People sometimes think that recovery from an eating disorder is all about weight, eating and activity—but this is not true. The real personal growth in therapy happens as you come to understand and effectively address the emotions, thoughts and circumstances that trigger your symptoms. People who recover from an eating disorder often say that, despite the misery, they would not choose to live their lives over without having had and recovered from an eating disorder. It is not the eating disorder they value; it is the wisdom they gain in the process of recovery that they would not do without.

A Patient's Perspective on Finding Healthy Ways to Tolerate Difficult Emotions:

Martin

For me, the best way to tolerate difficult emotions is to imagine them as clouds in the sky passing by, or water in a stream. I once read that if we don't hold on to them, emotions last about thirty seconds. These ideas help me to remember that emotions come and go. When these don't help, I clean the house, go for a long walk, do volunteer work, or help a friend. I also like to listen to music from the 1940s, 1950s or 1960s because of its childhood familiarity and the warmth of the recordings' quality.

Lynn

It is my belief that disordered eating and coping with difficult emotions are closely linked. If this is true, then in order to fully recover, one must learn to tolerate such feelings. Developing an awareness of these emotions is an important first step. Each individual will have to learn new ways to manage. Common 'tools' include distraction and self-soothing. I find that it is really helpful to remind myself what is truly important. I have found that tolerating difficult emotions is one of the most challenging parts of recovery but it is possible and it gets easier with time and practice.

Martin: My Recovery Story

DIAGNOSIS: BINGE EATING DISORDER

In my family, food is love. I was rarely made to feel as loved as I was when my German mom told me she had baked something especially for me. Refusing to eat seconds or thirds could hurt their feelings, and being a sensitive and obedient child, why would I want to do that? Besides, they were incredible bakers and the food tasted so good. It took more and more food to get that good feeling, and it led to binge eating.

When it came to food, my parents were pretty adventurous. They would take me on long car trips to try—wait for it—quiche Lorraine! Hey, that was daring back in 1970.… Eating "exotic" foods was a way of connecting with the places I read about and desperately wanted to visit. By my twenties, I was living in Paris. It was in France that I learned that good food and drink were an easy way for introverted me to connect with people who were happy to educate a "savage" like me. They could talk about French food history and traditions, as well as the best combinations of food. All I had to do was listen and eat. As my own knowledge of the subject grew, I would get lost in restaurant-size portions of food and tune out whoever was talking too much. This became a strategy I used whenever I was frustrated or bored with a dinner companion who talked too much. Gradually and without noticing, rapid overeating just became a way of life.

I was an introverted only child who much preferred his own company, happiest on my own in a corner reading, playing with my cat or my toy cars, or watching TV. Human relationships seemed so complicated, unpredictable and emotionally draining. I wasn't a resilient child. We moved every four years or so, which didn't help me to connect with others. I let things—totally innocent things—my family and friends did and said bother me long afterwards, sometimes for years. If I'm tired or stressed, I still run the risk of letting a few of them overwhelm me. Food wasn't unpredictable or critical. It would never make me feel uncomfortable. Or so I thought…

I had to change my attitude to my weight because years of yo-yo dieting had made me physically uncomfortable. It was a reflection of my inner anxiety, frustration and anger about who I was and how to live with other people. Dieting would fix everything, my attractiveness, my self-confidence, my outsider status. It would make being a gay man okay in largely straight world. I hated my job because I didn't think I could really be myself, but the pay and benefits were great, so I stayed with it for nearly thirty years. Dieting, then regaining the weight (and then some) shut my world down even further. I wouldn't go out, wouldn't date and my life became working, then going home, eating and bracing myself for the next work day. Weekends were spent eating and then lying comatose on the sofa.

Ultimately, staying the same was more painful than changing. I started this program about three years ago now, and it has been very beneficial because of the challenges it presented. The process has been more about shifting my thinking than about reaching a specific weight. I have hit those specific weights at least five times in my life. I was the same unhappy person, only thinner. All I did was treat the symptom, and not the cause. I had to work hard to overcome my resistance to change. It was hard to talk to myself in a positive, encouraging way and not roll my eyes or feel insincere. A friend suggested I look at a picture of myself as a child and imagine talking to that child the way I talk to my adult self. I was horrified to think of someone talking to a child that way. It has changed how I treat myself and others.

Many things have come very easily to me in my life, so if something was challenging, I would give up. I had to let go of all-or-nothing, black-and-white thinking. I had to accept that doing something was better than doing nothing, and the more I did the better things could be. At first, writing food journals and planning meals felt like a real chore. Once I came up with a list of six or seven healthful meals I like to eat for each of the seasons, recording and planning were easier.

Nowadays I get out the door, meet people and do things I would never have done before. I choose my dinner companions more wisely and focus on them rather than on the food. I don't worry about what people are thinking about me. I can see that, in almost all cases, people are too busy with their own thoughts to pay attention to me. I dress in bright colours and clothes that I would wear at any weight. It has given me a degree of peace I never thought possible, because I really understand that the most important person who was rejecting me was me. I've even begun to consider it possible that romance might not be out of the question, but it's still a struggle.

Am I completely recovered? No. The term seems to suggest I've learned everything I have to learn, which is absolutely not the case. Recovery is a process that will take the rest of my life. While I'm no longer a helpless captive to unhealthy long held ways of thinking and behaving, I must accept that these patterns are very old and ingrained and have the potential to catch me by surprise. It is only my belief that recovery is ongoing that helps to me remain mindful. The conscious act of being able to resist my first impulse is what allows healthier thoughts and behaviour to replace it and work towards a life that I believe is worth living.

Martin: What I Wanted for My Pictures

… something related to France might be appropriate. Perhaps one of Hector Guimard's elaborate art nouveau subway entrances … or … a Wallace Fountain….

An Artist's Perspective: A Note from Sharon

I tried to honour Martin's request by creating pages that relate to his travels in France. I wanted them to represent Martin's love of culture, design and good taste.

METROPOLITAIN

Lynn: My Recovery Story

DIAGNOSIS: ANOREXIA NERVOSA, BINGE EATING/PURGING TYPE

Hello. Welcome to my story. My name is Lynn and I am 43 years old. I am recovering from an eating disorder. I have been working at recovery for almost two years. It has not been an easy road but it has been worth it. I feel like I am close to being fully recovered but there are a few areas I need to fine tune.

My eating disorder began as a way for me to cope—of course I did not realize this at the time. My husband was in a job that caused him tremendous stress and our relationship was strained. I was working full time and trying to do everything at home. I felt like my world was falling apart. I was always stressed. At this time I began experiencing a lot of digestive issues. My doctor was not able to offer me guidance—I was told I had IBS.

I made the decision to go to a Naturopath in hopes of alleviating the discomfort I was experiencing. She instantly told me my symptoms were likely due to food intolerances and she advised me to start on an elimination diet. I soon became obsessed with what I could and could not eat. My diet gave me something to control. I had eliminated all gluten, dairy, eggs and raw vegetables. Weight started dropping and people noticed but I kept insisting that it was because of my new way of eating. As my weight continued dropping my Naturopath became concerned and recommended that I speak to someone at Danielle's Place—an eating disorder support center in Burlington. I was afraid to admit that I had a serious problem. I went to the support center shaking with anxiety. It was the first step for me on the road to recovery.

I connected with a wonderful woman at the center who helped me to acknowledge that I did indeed have an eating disorder and that I needed to get help. One of the hardest things I had to do was to admit to my husband, doctor, and my boss that I was struggling with an eating disorder. I decided to take a leave of absence from work. At the time, I truly believed that if I just had some time that I could focus on recover and fix things. It was not that easy. When I was off from work my eating disorder actually worsened—I was eating very little and began binging because I was starving and then purging came into the picture. As my eating disorder became more serious I realized that recovery was not going to be as simple as I thought. My doctor had referred me to various hospital treatment programs but the wait lists were at least 3 months long. I needed some support so I began a closed support group at Danielle's Place that ran one night a week. My therapist at the time mentioned that there was a private clinic in North York called Water-Stone, which offered full day treatment and had no wait list. The cost was more than I would be able to afford but upon contacting the clinic I was told they have a Foundation that grants funding to those in financial need. I began the process of filling in an intensive application form. To my surprise I was awarded a grant and after contacting the clinic I was scheduled to begin immediately.

This phase of recovery was hard. I cried every day. It was a very emotional experience. I felt gut busting fullness after every meal. I had to eat when I wasn't hungry. We ate dessert at lunch time. I was expected to continue eating according to my meal plan outside of the program hours. The treatment center became a really safe place to recover but out of those doors I was left on my own. I struggled to gain weight every week. Logically, I knew I had to gain the weight, I knew

I was dangerously thin but somehow seeing the number increase always caused me great anxiety. About halfway through my stay at WaterStone I was contacted by St. Joe's to take part in the Making Changes group. It would be perfect timing. I could finish at the clinic and as I transitioned back into life I could have a support group in place.

I think surrounding myself with supportive people was a key component in my recovery journey. When I was in the thick of the eating disorder I was alone—I lied, I avoided, I denied that I had a problem. Being in recovery was the polar opposite—I reached out to every resource that I could find and I leaned on whomever I could. One of the biggest obstacles for me along the way was my mood. I have had a long struggle with depression but it was manageable. About half way through my recovery, my mood took a real nose dive and I was struggling a lot. Everything seemed hard and I plateaued for a while. I worked with my psychiatrist to adjust my medications and after many changes I finally feel like the dark cloud is lifting.

Recovery has given me my life back. Life with an eating disorder isn't really living. I finally have energy. I can sleep. I enjoy meals with my family. My husband and I have grown closer. My kids have a healthy role model. I do still struggle at times with body image. I have settled at my 'set point'—which is a little higher than I would like—so I do have a hard time with self-acceptance. Recovery has not been an easy journey—it was a torturous path for me. At times I took detours and tried to hang on to the eating disorder. I used all of the supports that I could find and I feel blessed to have met so many wonderful supportive people as I worked on recovery.

Lynn: What I Wanted for My Pictures

As for the picture ... I find water very soothing ... something about seeing waves roll in and hearing it is so relaxing.

An Artist's Perspective: A Note from Sharon

How soothing is the water, and Lynn's request put me in mind of water swirling. I wanted to capture the freedom of undulating waves, not only in a body of water, but everywhere—bubbles and froth, all around. Reminiscent of the freedom from an eating disorder, when one is in recovery.

Recovery Theme 7

PICKING YOURSELF UP AND LEARNING FROM SETBACKS

A Therapist's Perspective on Picking Yourself Up and Learning from Setbacks: Michèle

Maybe you had been doing *so well* with not binge eating, and then a stressful weekend ended with you up at night binge eating the way you used to. Maybe you had been doing *such a good job* normalizing your eating, and then the scale reached a number you didn't think you could bear. Maybe you've worked *really hard* to stop purging, but visiting with family and eating more than you expected left you standing over the toilet. Or despite your commitment to stick to your goals, you found yourself sneaking off for another run or staying another hour at the gym. When you have a bad day (or a bad week!), it is hard not to feel discouraged and angry with yourself. You feel scared that you can't do this recovery thing. You may want to give up on yourself and give up on recovery. You have the thought that it would just be easier to go back to your eating disorder....

I often say that it doesn't take *perfection* to recover from an eating disorder; it takes *patience*, *persistence* and a *willingness to learn from your setbacks*. When things go wrong, you need to be patient with yourself. Recovery is hard. Even when you are truly trying, you will not be prepared for every trigger and you will not always have the energy or motivation to "do the right thing". Patience means you treat yourself with compassion. If you take the time to consider the circumstances of your setback, self-compassion will allow you to understand how your behavior "makes sense"—even if you might want it to be different next time. Recovery also takes persistence. You come back to treatment even if you had a bad week; you try again to be open to finishing the experiment and doing body image work; you get back to using the tools you've been taught. You decide that you will keep going. And finally, recovery takes a willingness to learn from setbacks. Recovery would be easy if life never got in the way. But recovery is all about learning how to handle stress, anxiety, loneliness, boredom, sadness and feeling bad about your body not being exactly what you want it to be, *without* turning to your eating disorder. If you are patient with yourself, and persistent in looking to recover, then setbacks are actually gifts. They might be difficult at the time, but in problem-solving each setback, you are a step closer to recovery. So when you have a setback, pick yourself up, give yourself a hug for having a hard day, and try to learn what the setback has to teach you.

A Patient's Perspective on
Picking Yourself Up and Learning from Setbacks:
Kaitlin

Setbacks will happen. There's no such thing as "perfect" recovery; you're riding a rollercoaster. Accept that you're moving forward even while headed downhill.

See each setback as the opportunity to learn. Think back to what led to this moment. What were you doing? Thinking? Feeling? Who did you speak to? If you can, write about what happened. Over time, you will see patterns in your setbacks that will help you overcome them.

Check in with yourself. Do you feel guilty, angry, anxious about what happened? Use this as the chance to practice self-compassion. Forgive yourself for having a bad day. I promise that you can still recover.

Nancy

Before recovery, setbacks led to bingeing—long periods of bingeing accompanied by beating myself up for failing again. The bingeing would only stop when I started my next sure-fire diet, which always led to a setback. It was a vicious cycle that never changed.

Due to recovery, that cycle finally changed. Setbacks still happen and always will, but now thanks to persistence and an awesome support system, there's no longer any bingeing or self-re-crimination. Now, after a setback, I find the right tool in my new skill set, apply it, forgive myself and keep on going.

Kaitlin: My Recovery Story

DIAGNOSIS: BULIMIA NERVOSA

I sometimes think of my eating disorder as a series of firsts. The first time I called myself fat. The first time I looked at a beautiful classmate and wished I were her. My first diet, and my frantic efforts to keep off the weight I had lost. The first binge that made me feel that I had completely lost control of myself. The first, awful time I forced myself to vomit.

Moments such as these stand out, but in reality my eating disorder was a constant, growing presence. As a competitive dancer, I grew up inside the mirrored walls of a studio, where I could constantly observe and compare myself to the girls around me. I prided myself as being an accomplished dancer, physically fit, and smaller than my peers. These parts of my identity became threatened when I underwent hip surgery at age 15, and I immediately sought to maintain my sense of self in any way that I could. Eating dinner in the hospital following my operation, I remember thinking, "I'd better watch what I eat." I pushed my half eaten dinner aside.

Though surgery did not precede all the firsts of my eating disorder, the chronic pain and decreased physical activity that followed this event exacerbated my body consciousness. Thus began the cycle of weight loss and gain that would follow me through my remaining high school years and into university. I became obsessed with controlling my weight through diet and exercise, and associated my size with success in other areas in life. I saw skinnier periods as times where I was happier, funnier, prettier, smarter, pain free; a "better" version of myself, in control of all meaningful aspects of my life. Episodes of weight loss were inevitably followed by binges and weight gain, which I interpreted as failures of my motivation. During these times, I perceived myself as a poor student, boring friend, and unprincipled young woman. As school became more demanding and life became more complex, it became increasingly important that I remain the better, smaller version of myself. The actions I took to maintain this self became progressively more extreme. I became sicker and less able to control the eating disorder's negative impact on my life. I became depressed and anxious. I withdrew from all my courses.

Like the disorder itself, I see recovery as a list of firsts. Firsts such as trusting someone else, my sister, with my secret; saying, "I have an eating disorder," out loud for the very first time. Making it through a day, week, month without a single episode of purging. Attending my first group therapy session. Creating and following a balanced meal plan. Ordering a slice of pizza. Wearing a fitted shirt on a day that I felt bloated. Getting into bed at the end of the day and realizing that I had not worried about my appearance at all.

No one first can be said to mark the moment that I began to recover, and I cannot remember a clear division between sickness and wellness. Moments of recovery often occurred at times when my eating disorder was at its worst. In 2012, I began therapy; I also began vomiting multiple times a day. In 2013, there were days when I liked the body that I saw in the mirror; there were also days when I cried because I had regained 25 pounds and my pants no longer fit. In 2014, I relapsed and was quite sick for several months; following this, I did not experience any symptoms for a long period of time. The fluidity of the line between disordered and recovered has been difficult for me to accept. I was sure that there would be an objective end point to my eating disorder, and that I would be recovered when I had been symptom free for months and years.

For me, recovery has not meant complete abandonment of my eating disordered self. Recovery has meant accepting that if I keep ice cream in my freezer, I may eat more of it in one sitting than I'd like to, and that the carton may be gone in a matter of days. Recovery has meant that I may feel anxious when I eat restaurant food for an entire week while traveling, and that I may feel guilty if I still choose to eat dessert on the day that I return home. Recovery continues to mean that one of the reasons that I engage in physical activity is that it helps me look my best. However, I no longer experience the sense of precariousness that dominated my eating disorder. I feel secure in the knowledge that a day or week of overeating will not lead me down a path of weight gain or disordered eating. I am motivated by factors other than my appearance to work out and lead a healthy lifestyle. I am recovered because my eating disorder has no say in the decisions I make and the values that define the person I am today.

Though rare, I still occasionally binge, and I have purged during this calendar year. Though it bothers me that these symptoms have not completely disappeared, I do not believe that they make me eating disordered. I simply have not lived all the firsts of recovery. I would love to go an entire year without purging, but I accept that this may never happen. In recovering, I have seen that imperfection can have value, and have learned to forgive myself for my limitations.

My recovery was shaped by the support I received from my wonderful psychologist and care team, the strong women who comprised my therapy group, and my fantastic family and friends. Their guidance, combined with my trust in the therapeutic process, was essential to my recovery. However, recovery is individual. It is impossible to replicate someone else's version of wellness. It was not until I recognized that I had to define my own recovery that I was finally able to shed my eating disorder and see myself as well.

Kaitlin: What I Wanted for My Pictures

The triquetra—a Celtic symbol for "balance". While recovering, I constantly had to remind myself to strive for balance in all areas of life as I worked towards overcoming my perfectionist tendencies to live a more realistic, healthy lifestyle. I actually drew this symbol on my wrist daily for about three months as a reminder to continue working towards this goal! This symbol always leaps into my mind as representative of the time when I was recovering from my eating disorder.

An Artist's Perspective: A Note from Sharon

I definitely knew I had to put in Kaitlin's Celtic triquetra as it held so much meaning for her. Although I did not include Irish dancing customs, I created an oak tree that is very symbolic in Celtic folklore, as it represents strength and endurance which are important attributes needed to recover from an eating disorder.

Nancy: My Recovery Story

DIAGNOSIS: BINGE EATING DISORDER

I was born into a family that struggled with obesity their entire lives. I learned from a very young age that in order to be a good person and deserve the good things in life, you had to be thin and attractive. You had to meet society's standard of beauty and that wasn't me. I was already overweight by the time I was 6. My family was continuously on the yoyo diet rollercoaster. My sister and I were enrolled in Weight Watchers when I was 12 and she was 11. We were the only children there and my family wasn't there with us. That's just the first of the diet programs that I can remember.

My teenage years were even more intense when it came to the drive to lose weight—my parents didn't want us to experience the peer difficulties that they had had in high school, so there was a lot of pressure to lose. Incentives were offered, too, such as $1 per pound lost, and later $5 and then $10 per pound lost. But, nothing worked for very long. Diet plans, incentives, pressure and criticism—they led to initial success followed by weight gain, always. I recall during dieting periods, sneaking food and money to buy junk food for my earliest binges. When I went away to University, I was suddenly in total control of my food choices for the first time in my life. This is when the binges became a much more frequent occurrence and the yo-yo dieting continued. The pressure to conform to a certain look and a certain size was still very high in university.

Nothing really changed over the course of my twenties, thirties, and forties, except that I kept gaining weight—I struggled and struggled with it, trying so hard to get down to that magic number. I never got there. Every time I started a new diet, I had that initial success but it never lasted. I would plateau and then start bingeing and gaining. I tried every program I could find, often more than once: Weight Watchers, Jenny Craig, Slim Fast, Overeater's Anonymous, Dr. Atkins, and every popular fad diet that came along. I tried to have bariatric surgery twice but was declined both times. After the second time, I spent over $21,000 for lap band surgery. It was 2009, I was 42 and over 400 pounds. At only 4' 11", I was having a lot of mobility trouble and other health issues. I felt absolutely sure that this was the solution to my lifelong weight problem. But, again, the pattern remained the same. After an initial loss, I plateaued and didn't lose anymore. I was in such despair. I didn't know what else to do—I felt like I'd tried everything. After the lap band surgery, I alternated mainly between bingeing and Dr. Atkins. The periods of bingeing were longer and the attempts at dieting were fewer.

Visits to my family doctor were avoided as much as possible. He put pressure on me to lose weight every single time I went to see him. In 2014, he referred me to the bariatric clinic again and I started the process to hopefully get on the list for gastric bypass surgery this time. Over the years, my attitude towards the bypass surgery changed—at first, I was judgmental of people who had it. I still believed that willpower was all that was needed to become the perfect weight and I just had to work harder at it. I thought the operation was a cop out. As time passed and my desperation grew, the surgery began to look more attractive. It became the magic bullet I needed if I was ever to reach my crazy, unattainable goal. The lap band surgery seemed a perfect substitute, and when I didn't succeed, the bypass surgery still seemed like the quick fix I needed.

My recovery began in 2014 when I was assessed at the bariatric clinic and diagnosed with binge eating disorder. I was floored—in all the years I'd been battling and struggling, it had never crossed my mind that I had an eating disorder. I was just a failure with no willpower. I was referred to a binge eating disorder group, Cognitive Behaviour Therapy, and there I learned so much about how my body works and my disorder. I learned skills that allowed me to normalize my eating and stop bingeing. It was very hard to accept that I would never be able to lose all my excess weight through dieting—it was devastating to understand that dieting was part of the problem and not the solution. In our society, weight loss programs and products are a multi-billion dollar industry—so many people like me trying to find the magic bullet that'll get them to that perfect number and solve all the problems in their lives. Some days, I still find myself reacting to a commercial for a program or product that promises to melt off my excess pounds. Then I remember the truth and stick to trying to eat all my food groups in their correct ratios and enjoying a life where I can eat without shame and without drastic restrictions. I'm back on the path to bariatric surgery again—fourth time's the charm! I'm able now to understand that the gastric bypass is another tool in my life to help me live healthier and more comfortably in my skin, it's not the magic solution. As a result, the bariatric doctor is willing to support me in this choice. In the meantime, I try to live each day feeding my body and accepting it at whatever weight it is, because whatever weight it is, I'm still a good person.

An Artist's Perspective: A Note from Sharon

Nancy's request was so easy to fill. The pictures are of cats. Who doesn't love cats? Even if they live in trees like owls....

Recovery Theme 8

LETTING THOSE CLOSE TO YOU SUPPORT YOU

A Therapist's Perspective on Letting Those Close to You Support You: Michèle

Should you tell your parents? Should you tell your friend? What about your partner? Is it a good idea to tell others in your life about your eating disorder? We know that eating disorders thrive in secrecy, so doesn't it make sense to talk about your experience? As you might expect, we typically see it as a very positive step when you decide to open up about your eating disorder to those you trust, and those close to you. Usually it is a sign that you are preparing for change. In telling others, however, it is important to understand that they often feel honoured that you have confided in them and assume that you are looking for their support. And they will assume that you are looking for their support to *recover*.

If you don't feel safe to open up to others in your life, sometimes therapy (especially group therapy) can be the one place you can open up and be supported by others who understand your eating disorder. If you are able to confide in people in your life, it is usually necessary to give them guidance in how, and how not, to be supportive. Often, the worry about telling others is that they will either be uncomfortable, or they will be intrusive. The best outcome is that you have someone who tells you they support you and asks what you would find helpful. Regardless of how your loved one reacts, you can still make it clear that you have made the decision to get help, that you want to be the one responsible for making changes, and that you are telling them because you hope they will provide you with support when you ask for it. People who recover often credit those close to them for getting them through the difficult times in recovery. Loved ones encourage you when you have doubts. They push you to keep trying when you are thinking of giving up. They hold you accountable. They give you rides to therapy. They take you to the hospital. They celebrate your successes. They may sometimes drive you crazy, but they are often one of your most important reasons to recover. Recovery is going to be hard at times—letting those close to you support you can make all the difference.

A Patient's Perspective on
Letting Those Close to You Support You: Catherine

My eating disorder was one of the darkest holes I've experienced and I wouldn't wish that upon anyone. But it gave me one of the best lessons of my life: I had people around me that truly cared and wanted to help, they just didn't know how. I began to speak to them, tell them my biggest barriers and my hardest thoughts and in exchange I got to experience so much love and support. It was no wonderland and it was the hardest hole to crawl back out of.

Cara-Lea

It can be hard to accept help, even harder to ask for help … but allowing the people closest to you to support and help you isn't just useful for recovery, it is absolutely necessary. The changes you need to make can impact many areas of your life and if the people around you aren't active participants, they can either passively or actively sabotage you.

Catherine: My Recovery Story

DIAGNOSIS: OTHER SPECIFIED FEEDING AND EATING DISORDER, PURGING DISORDER

Hi, my name is Catherine and I want to share a little bit about myself and my battle with an eating disorder. Growing up I wasn't liked very much. I was teased, ostracized, picked on, beat up, had my things stolen from my classroom desk, and was aimed at in sports. To this day I couldn't tell you why I wasn't liked; I am pretty shy and pretty quiet until you get to know me; I was taught—and still go by—the motto of being nice even if someone isn't nice to me; I try and help others when I can; and I tried hard in school, and I played competitive sports—you could say I am a bit of a perfectionist. I also come from a very loving and high achieving family; my father is a surgeon, my mother is an entrepreneur with several hundred employees, and both of my older siblings were in VP level positions by 26. I felt as though I was standing in pretty large shadows. My parents would never pressure me to be a high achiever, they are **so** supportive they would be proud of **anything** that I chose to become, but because I believed so strongly **my own** perceptions of standing in their high achieving shadows, being bullied really socialized me to internalize the idea that I just wasn't "good enough" (I put that in quotations because if I am being honest I still couldn't tell you what exactly "good enough" means or looks like and who really gets to decide that sort of thing).

I guess somewhere along the line of being bullied I thought maybe if I was thin enough, controlled enough, smart enough, or pretty enough that would make it better. That would fix it and I would "fit in". I cannot express how desperately I wanted to "fit in" (don't really know how to define that either)—I was **miserable**. So, I began to control food intake, skip meals, and lose a little weight—not enough for people to really notice. Never in my mind at that time did I believe I was "sick". I continued to control my food from Grade 9 through Grade 12 but the bullying never changed.

Then I went to university. I was so **excited!** I had a new opportunity, a clean slate, to make friends and to be "good enough". And then in my first year of university I was raped. My excitement was shattered. I didn't know how to tell anyone, so I didn't. I dealt with the PTSD by commanding significant control over my food intake and became anorexic. When I couldn't control myself I purged. I had my eating disorder for 10 years and went through therapy more than once. I felt like I was drowning but was unwilling to call the lifeboat and too proud to admit it when I saw the lifeboat (therapy). I could see the worry in the eyes of my family and my friends but I couldn't let go, I isolated myself. I became my own ostracizer. I eventually spoke to another woman who had been assaulted and saw her strength in the ownership of her assault. She didn't let one person derail her life. In that moment I realized that there is **no pride in struggling** and there's **no shame in seeking help**. So I did.

I spoke with a therapist on a weekly basis and I continued to do that for years. I spoke to her not only about my rape and my PTSD symptoms, but also about my crippling fear of failure and not "measuring up" or "fitting in". I was ready to throw myself at any career path I thought would look good in the eyes of others—I applied to medical schools, law schools, and masters programs. It didn't matter that I had no interest in doing that occupation, I would do it just to finally be "good enough". I had **no idea** what I liked, was interested in, or what I wanted to do. I spent so many years trying to measure up to others that I had almost forgotten to have my own interests, passions, and hobbies. Writing it now makes it sound easy but I struggled for almost two years trying to figure out my path.

At the same time through therapy I was able to weight restore—which was a terrifying experience and ended up far better than I was expecting (come to think of it, I don't really know what I was expecting, in my head I would just continue to gain weight and thought eventually I would just explode and looking back it's a bit ridiculous really)—and finally let go of the control that I had over food. In reality I was letting go of **the control that the food had over me**. Believe me, it wasn't a walk in the park or letting go and walking away a different person the very next day. It was **work**. It was some of the hardest work I have ever had to do, but it was by far the most rewarding so far.

I began to explore things that I might like, started to learn a little about the person that I had lost in the shadows and control. I did a second degree once I found something that I really truly enjoyed learning about and then in my last year struggled again to try and figure out what I wanted to do. During my thesis I developed a crippling sickness that lasted over a year. I managed to get my thesis done while in hospital and begin working on grad school applications at the same time. I was a varsity athlete who used to be sponsored and who was reduced to being unable to walk without pain or get up without help. I was put on a course of steroids to see if that could help and with them I gained 22 pounds. As a recovered eating disorder patient that was hard. It took every fibre of my being not to "fix it" in my old way. I couldn't exercise and I couldn't stop gaining weight. I woke up in the mornings to look into a closet of things I couldn't fit into and feel desperate. I was exhausted, in more pain than I had ever experienced, and gaining weight. My worst nightmare. I write this now as I am beginning to be able to walk and participate in things again, I am in less pain, and I did not fix my weight. I used the healthy techniques I had been taught and was calling to speak to someone on a regular basis, whether it was my family, my friends, or a professional. I did everything I could to stop myself from falling back down that hole and the biggest help was my support network.

Being recovered, to me, doesn't mean there is never temptation to try and control your weight or "just do it this one time" because it is some sort of "special" circumstance. There is. That temptation to fix my body stayed for a year. What stopped me from engaging in it was the fear of falling back and the immense amount of support around me that was bringing me up—no matter how hard I put myself down. I still wanted to be "good enough" and to "fit in" but I believe there is more merit to doing it as me, just the way I am and I cannot thank my family and my friends enough for giving me the opportunity to see that (and I still really don't know what fitting in or being good enough means … so, ya know, if anyone figures it out please let me know!).

I wish each of you the very best in your recovery. I cannot tell you what it will be like, it's different for everyone. But I truly believe that being recovered is worth every bit of effort you have to put in along the way, regardless of how hard it is to muster (I know). Each and every one of you deserves to get to be you: To be free to be happy and to do it in your own skin. It's possible and it is worth it. You won't believe me now (I wouldn't have believed someone if they told me this when I had my eating disorder) but you won't realize how controlling and consuming the eating disorder is and how much happier you can be without it. I hope each of you take the opportunity to **be you**!

Catherine: What I Wanted for My Pictures

For the art that goes with my story I was thinking maybe having people linking arms …

An Artist's Perspective: A Note from Sharon

For Catherine all I could think of was how much support she was provided during her recovery. What came to mind were two images. One of two friends with arms around each other's shoulders providing encouragement and support. The other picture was of women, smiling, who as Catherine would say, look happy in their own skin.

Cara-Lea: My Recovery Story

DIAGNOSIS: OTHER SPECIFIED FEEDING OR EATING DISORDER, BINGE EATING DISORDER OF LOW FREQUENCY

I have had an eating disorder for as long as I can remember. Food was used against me in childhood as a form of emotional abuse. I was also body shamed, physically abused and bullied from a very young age. I started seeking comfort in food from as young an age as I can remember and sometime in my early teens I began bingeing on a regular basis. When I was in university I had some very good friends who saw that I was very unwell and made me go to the counselling centre on campus to ask for help. I was diagnosed with depression at that point and my path towards healing and recovery began.

Over the many years since that diagnosis, I have been through doctors, medications and therapists … some of which truly helped, some didn't. I ended up with an extensive list of diagnoses, but I learned to not allow myself to be defined by them. Rather I took each as a chance to know myself more fully and a chance to move towards a more emotionally and mentally healthy version of myself. That being said, I spent all of those years I was working on my mental health also struggling with my weight and my physical health. I lost varying amounts of weight through varying programs. At one point I lost 120 lbs. and got to the lowest adult weight of my life. Every single time I gained the weight back. I hated the fact I couldn't keep the weight off. I felt like no matter how hard I worked on my mental health, I was still failing because I couldn't get thin and stay there. So in 2014 I told my therapist I wanted to sort out my issues around food so I could lose weight and keep it off. We did a variety of work, exposure therapies, mindfulness/meditation, talk therapy. It all helped me get to a place where I could finally talk about my bingeing, and I was diagnosed with Binge Eating Disorder. I was then referred to the Eating Disorders Program at St. Joseph's Hospital.

After six months of work with the Making Changes program, I am not bingeing. I want to say I feel like I am 100% recovered, but I do still think of turning to food in times of stress … the big difference now is that I don't actually do it. Perhaps that means I am 95% recovered. The hardest part for me during recovery and still is that I genuinely love food. Bingeing was pleasurable for me, until it made me feel sick and ashamed. Sometimes I miss that feeling of throwing myself into a pile of food. Sometimes I worry that I could accidentally slip back into a binge because I'm just enjoying eating something so much that I lose control. I think it will always be with me in some way, but I also know now I have support and skills that if I do slip, I can recover.

The program has genuinely changed my life. Not only have I been able to accept my body as it is, I have begun to truly embrace it. I have stopped bingeing and learned coping strategies for the triggers that used to cause me to binge. I have more confidence, feel more comfortable in my own skin and it feels wonderful to not feel shame about my body or about food. My relationship with food and eating is still a work in progress. I suspect it always will be … but now I'm far more prepared to handle it.

Cara-Lea: What I Wanted for My Pictures

I have 2 thoughts on this ... first would be a depiction of a plus sized woman doing yoga ... second would be a view of mountains with maybe a lake or river. These two ideas could even be combined.

An Artist's Perspective: A Note from Sharon

For Cara-Lea I wanted to show a person doing yoga who is comfortable with who she is. To honour her request I have included a mountain in the background. Her second picture is of a small island with trees, to remind us all that we are not islands unto ourselves, but need the nourishment of those around us to continue to flourish, and not to be afraid to ask for support.

Recovery Theme 9

LEARNING TO ACCEPT YOURSELF, IMPERFECT AS YOU ARE

A Therapist's Perspective on Learning to Accept Yourself, Imperfect as You Are: Michèle

One of the questions you may have is *why* you developed an eating disorder. We know that part of the answer is unique to you; different life events may have made you vulnerable in particular ways. Research has also suggested that, as someone who has developed an eating disorder, you may have temperamental traits you were born with that put you at risk.

The traits that are part of the temperament of a person vulnerable to developing an eating disorder are traits we associate with perfectionism. Perfectionism is not so much about *being* perfect as it is about the anxiety of making a mistake or falling short. Perfectionism means having a strong desire to meet the highest standards in your own and other people's eyes. Perfectionism means having self-esteem that is fragile because you are never sure that who you are, or what you have achieved, is good enough. When you have an eating disorder, perfectionism is powerfully centred on the worry that your weight, shape and appearance are not good enough. Recovery from an eating disorder means taking the risk of being your natural self. With respect to appearance, this means taking the risk of being whatever weight you are as a person living a healthy lifestyle. Recovery means that you learn to recognize, and then quiet the self-critical voice. Recovery means doing planned exposures where you learn to face the world with confidence in a body you don't believe is perfect. In achieving this, you begin the work of accepting yourself; believing that you are good enough, imperfect though you may be.

A Patient's Perspective on
Learning to Accept Yourself, as Imperfect as You Are:
Katie

So to you, the reader: Don't give up. You are being challenged. You are brave, you are strong, and you are beautiful. Wherever you are in recovery please know that it will get better. Your weight is not your worth, you are so much more than that. Take the time you used to spend on your eating disorder for fun instead. Find what makes you happy—truly happy—and let it consume you. You might have people or things that you need to let go of, and know it is OK to let go. Remember to give people time. Be patient with them, and with yourself. Try again, and keep going. Good luck.

Karen

What do I love about my imperfect self? Not one of us is perfect, but what I often have to remember is this: "I am perfect to those that love me, and all of my flaws are what make me the person I am today. Learning to love myself was the hardest thing I had to do. But I do—I love myself just as I am and I accept my imperfections as the road map of my success!" There is that line in John Legend's song, "All of Me": "I love all of your perfect imperfections!" Every inch of me is me—regardless of size, colour of my hair, whether I wear glasses or a bathing suit—and I've have learned to love all of my perfect imperfections!

Katie: My Recovery Story

DIAGNOSIS: ANOREXIA NERVOSA, RESTRICTING TYPE

I did not realize that I had an eating disorder until it had already happened. I suddenly found myself skinny and alone. In Grade 12, I was diagnosed with an illness that forced me to quit sports. I gained some weight. In my first year of university and throughout my second, I became consumed and obsessed with the shame of not being what I thought was expected of me. I, and everyone else, are made to believe that we will not be wanted, not be loved, if we are not beautiful, and that beauty is on the outside. The way that the world made me feel about myself made me so determined to be thin that nothing else mattered. I ran miles and miles and ate nothing. I told myself I was weak when I was hungry, and I was weak when I ate. I spent hours looking at magazines and recipes, obsessed with food. I convinced myself that I just loved to run, that I was an athlete, and that the lifestyle that I led was the right one. My clothes stopped fitting, and it fed the fire. I wore my size zeroes like medals. Now that I was skinny, I had to maintain it. So I kept going.

But I was unhappy. It didn't make sense. I had what was the most important, the only important thing. I cried most days. I did not feel like going out with my friends, and I was mean to them. I shut everyone out. I binged in secret and then punished myself by starving and running. I was so sad and so lonely but it wasn't my fault, it was everyone else's. I was doing what was right, and everyone else was doing it wrong. It is hard for me to think of this person that I had become.

I feel lucky that my eating disorder only took a year of my life. When I finally went to outpatient recovery, everything started to make sense. The things that I learned about eating disorders made so much sense that I cannot believe I didn't see it before. The summer after second year, I went to work at my childhood camp. I put myself into nature, into having fun, and tried to forget about everything else. I returned to school in September with a new mindset, new determination. I was horrified by the mess I had created, the people that my eating disorder had hurt, and the damage it had caused. My friends forgave me; they slowly let me back into their lives. It took time, and patience. It took understanding that people do not always know how to deal with something like this, and that it is not their fault. That they cannot see that you are suffering from the shame you feel, only that you have become a depressed, angry person. I did not give up running, but I gave up what it used to mean to me. I ran again sometimes because it felt good, because it brings me joy, not because it produced a number on a scale. It is amazing how much extra time you have to enjoy yourself when you aren't worrying about your body.

The moment when I truly began to recover was when I realized that what I look like is not what makes me beautiful. Beauty, in fact, has nothing to do with my size, shape, or anything else that can be seen on Facebook. Happiness is beautiful. Friendship is beautiful. Laughing is beautiful. Strength of character is more important than weight. Why do I want to turn the heads of strangers, anyways? I realized that I wanted to be valued by things that could not be measured. The world is too amazing, and life is too short, to worry about things that will not matter in a week—things that should not matter in order to be loved.

There are things that I had to sacrifice to make it through. When I examined my core beliefs and I became aware of my own happiness, I began to realize what it was that may have caused this thing, and what could still contribute to it. There are relationships that I realized I should not and could not continue if I truly wanted to get better. Throughout treatment I became an expert in my eating disorder, and began to see my old self in a family member. The excessive exercise, binging and starving, loss of control and the unhappiness that crept in all too often. It hurts me that she refused to get help, not just for her but for me. It is hard to see her suffer the way that I suffered. I know that detaching myself from her is the best way to protect myself, at least for now.

I remind myself to be brave all the time. Recovery is hard. The mind is a strange thing. I still have days where I feel like if my body could just look a certain way, maybe that person would like me, or maybe I would be more confident. But then I compare skinny me to happy me, and I know I have made the right choice.

Katie: What I Wanted for My Pictures

I guess for the picture if Sharon wanted to add something to do with nature/the outdoors/the forests and lakes ... this was a part of my recovery so I thought might be relevant.

An Artist's Perspective: A Note from Sharon

It is not surprising that trees and nature were themes. I wanted to honour Katie's requests with a stand of trees that represent nourishment, transformation and more importantly, liberation. The string of leaves was to capture how trees, nature, and all of us are intertwined in our human journey.

Karen: My Recovery Story

DIAGNOSIS: BINGE EATING DISORDER (POST-BARIATRIC SURGERY)

I fell down the rabbit hole—well, at least it felt like I did! I can't quite remember exactly when, but it's been many years of chasing the FAD diet; Jenny Craig, Nutrisystem, Weight Watchers (about 12 times), the soup diet, the grapefruit diet, raw, vegetarian—I've done them all. I finally decided that the life of fad diets just wasn't for me. I was so depressed and miserable and felt like there was no light at the end of the tunnel that I ended up in my family physician's office asking for help. That was the day she referred me for gastric bypass surgery. I was pretty sure she was jumping for joy in her chair—she had seen me at my best and for many years at my worst. Things seemed to be looking up—change was in the air!

In 2009 I had the surgery. From beginning to end—that included two weeks of liquid starvation before surgery—I lost approximately 120 lbs. However, when you think something is going to be easy, it never really is. The dreaded plateau happened and I couldn't lose anymore, even though in my own mind what I was seeing still needed improvement. I needed to lose MORE—and it wasn't happening. That's when the depression came back—and also donuts, cake, chips, chocolate and many other forms of great sugary snacks, into my life. I wasn't eating that much of it—I could barely finish a donut—but still, to someone who has had the surgery—that donut was like having 12. I just binged, the depression was taking over, I was gaining weight instead of losing it, and I got even more depressed. The more I ate the crap, the more depressed and helpless I was feeling.

I knew something was wrong. I addressed it at the [bariatric] clinic but they just said, "Well, what are you eating? Stop eating that, get back on track!" Well, okay, I can do that—but what about my depression? I landed back at my family docs' office—that's when she sent me to eating disorder treatment—that first appointment was a real eye opener. During the course of therapy I managed to learn some things about myself I didn't know before—that I was a great person, I am lovable, I'm beautiful just as I am—and I'm a binge eater! Yes, I am all of those things—and I'm also human.

Since going through the treatment and CBT—I fell on some hard times. I've had so many health setbacks because of the surgery—the major one being I can't absorb any iron, B_{12} and my ferritin is always low—and have since discovered I'm anemic. The feeling of chronic pain and fatigue, vertigo, constant headaches, restless legs—I felt like I was chained to a chair and bed every day all day. I wasn't getting any exercise. Thanks to a great specialist who took the time to SEE me and HEAR me, I have since started IV Iron treatments and am looking forward to getting back on the treadmill, maybe do a little Zumba and preparing to do the around-the-bay 5k next year—I'm hoping to run/walk!! My other setback was the death of my mother. I took care of her right up until her last hospital admit and her death. Since that time depression set in again. I fell off the wagon. But, since then I've managed to take control of my eating and my thoughts and can move forward every day for the last seven months with NO binges. There is light at the end of the tunnel—even if you slip a little and have to take another run through—you will survive—you GOT this!!

My advice to those reading going through all that I did is this: "Remember you are beautiful, you are amazing, you can do anything, YOU are in control of you—and yes, you can still have *a* cookie!!"

Karen: What I Wanted for My Pictures

My life right now is absorbed around photography, painting, travelling (something I never really did before because I was too embarrassed to get on a plane) and my music—I teach folks to play the great highland bagpipe.

An Artist's Perspective: A Note from Sharon

I loved the fact Karen wanted to incorporate bagpipes in her picture—how original! Likewise, I wanted to capture her love of photography through a page of vintage cameras.

Recovery Theme 10

CHOOSING JOY AND CONNECTION OVER CONTROL AND PERFECTION

A Therapist's Perspective on Choosing Joy and Connection over Control and Perfection: Michèle

We are all born with temperaments and, in my opinion, every temperament has its strengths and vulnerabilities. Researchers have been careful to explain that many of the temperamental traits associated with becoming eating disordered—concern over others' approval; persistence; being detail oriented; preferring predictability over change—are the same traits that make people successful in life. Other traits related to eating disorders, such as impulsivity and emotional intensity, can also be related to spontaneity and passion. I like to think of temperament as a horse you are given at birth. If you have an eating disorder, you have been given a big, beautiful, black stallion (in my imagination) of a temperament. It is an amazingly powerful horse that can do wonderful things. But it can also drag you all over the countryside if you let it. The task of recovery is to figure out how to manage your horse: when to give it the freedom to run, and when to rein it in. To recover, you have to come to know your horse well.

In recovery, you will have to decide what principles will guide your life. Your temperament will push you to "do your best". The desire to "do your best" may extend to many areas of your life: your performance as a student or employee; your performance as a daughter or son; your performance as a mother or father; your performance as a friend. When you keep the focus on doing your best, the big, black stallion that is your temperament is being given free rein. You may accomplish many things; but you are at risk of neglecting your own well-being. People who recover from an eating disorder often conclude that the principle of "balance" must guide their lives if they are to remain well. To recover, you must balance your desire to choose the healthiest foods with the desire to join in socially and have pleasure in what you eat. To recover, you must balance your desire to achieve a "perfect" (or even "acceptable") body with your need to live a life that feels tolerable. To recover, you must balance your desire to please others with your need to take care of yourself. To recover, you must balance your desire to impress others with your need to honour your own interests and preferences in the choices you make. To recover, you must balance your desire to be successful with your need to attend to the relationships you have with the people you love. Managing the horse that is your temperament is to always be working at striking the right *balance*: knowing when to choose joy and connection over your natural inclination toward control and perfection. This is the larger task of recovery.

A Patient's Perspective on
Choosing Joy and Connection over Control and Perfection:
Michelle

Having an eating disorder is exhausting. There's no energy or room to enjoy life to its fullest. Even though it doesn't feel like it, there is an amazing world full of so much joy following recovery. When things seem impossible and you want to give up, focus on the life you want ... your future goals, your family, and your career ... whatever it is that you want to achieve out of life, and think about the likelihood of you having this life with an eating disorder. I promise that you will never regret choosing recovery and a life that goes far beyond your eating disorder.

Julie

We are human. Humans are not perfect. None of us are perfect. Yet in a world filled with so much focus on being perfect how can we not be hard on ourselves when we fail? It starts with self-love. Love yourself enough to take actions necessary to find true happiness, to set a high standard for relationships, and when things don't go as planned, to forgive yourself. Pick yourself up, dust yourself off and do it all over again. Be kind to you. If you don't who will? By doing this you are choosing joy over control and perfection.

Michelle: My Recovery Story

DIAGNOSIS: ANOREXIA NERVOSA, BINGE EATING/PURGING TYPE, AND BULIMIA NERVOSA

I struggled with an eating disorder for approximately 17 years before I considered myself to be recovered. At 8 years old, I remember having body image issues, and by 10 I began to starve myself. I was diagnosed with anorexia which went on for years before I started a vicious cycle of starving, binging and laxative abuse. At 14 years old, merely days after I started outpatient treatment, I was hospitalized for my eating disorder. Once home, I continued outpatient individual and group therapy and things seemed to be getting better. I discontinued treatment although I still hadn't dealt with many of the body image issues that remained. In the years to follow, I engaged myself in a world of fitness where I hid behind the image of a "healthy lifestyle." It was anything but healthy. I was constantly dieting, bingeing, purging and exercising excessively. I went through periods, depending on what was happening in my personal life, where things improved but it was always just temporary. My eating disorder always seemed to "haunt" me and I began to believe that it was just something that was going to struggle with indefinitely. However, in my late twenties, I sought treatment again. I was ready to move forward.

There's no question that recovering from an eating disorder was the most difficult thing I have ever done. Letting go of the control and trusting my body seemed impossible most days. I was so used to counting every calorie, measuring out every meal, and controlling every pound of myself. Learning to trust that my body would respond reasonably to healthy eating without making me "fat" was, without a doubt, the most difficult part for me about the recovery process. I remember having many meltdowns over my clothes getting tighter or the number on the scale changing regardless of how subtle it was. There were many times where I took one step forward and two steps back because I felt like my body was working against me. The constant anxiety was overwhelming. However, what troubled me more than any of these things was the thought that I would never escape my eating disorder. That's what kept me going. I continually reminded myself that if I didn't change something, then I would live the rest of my life "stuck". I would never move forward and achieve the things that I wanted out of life the most. Using counter-thoughts was a huge part of recovery for me.

Looking back over my experience, I feel like readiness is a huge part of the recovery process. Although I found recovery to be difficult, I knew more than anything that I wanted to get well. I was simply "done" with my eating disorder and was ready to seek treatment and make changes.

For people recovering from an eating disorder, I think it's important for them to know that it's OK to not like the recovery process. It's hard and there are going to be days where they just don't trust it. I had many of these days … but if they just dig deep and keep moving forward, eventually it really does get better. I know it sounds clichéd to say "don't give up" but fighting through recovery was the best thing I've ever done. Recovery changed my life in ways that I never thought possible. I don't wake up each morning rushing to the scale. I don't obsess about food anymore and when I look at myself in the mirror, I don't judge my body anymore. I am a mother to a beautiful baby boy and a wife to a wonderful man. I am a daughter, a sister and a friend. I am no longer defined by my curves or the number on the scale. I exercise when I feel like it and I eat for health and wellness—not to control my weight. During my eating disorder, I never thought in a million years that I would get to this point. I attribute this to treatment, readiness, persistence and a lot of strength. So for those struggling … no matter how hopeless things feel, there really is a life for them beyond their eating disorder.

An Artist's Perspective: A Note from Sharon

Michelle asked for trees, which is not surprising given the symbolism of trees. The trees I drew for Michelle were solid and firm, to represent her strength, stability, connectedness and her new-found joy of life.

Julie: My Recovery Story

DIAGNOSIS: BINGE EATING DISORDER

At the tender and impressionable age of 13 I met a boy. He was tall, blond, athletic, handsome and three years older than me. He said he loved me. I loved him. I spent eight years with him. Eight years of being told I'm not good enough, pretty enough, strong enough. Controlled. Emotionally and mentally abused. Several times I tried to break up with him only to be told no one will love me like him and if I leave him he will kill himself. These were heavy words for a young woman. I was afraid. What if he was right? Food became my comfort. Food never treated me badly. Food told me I was perfect. I learned to hide the treats and binge when my boyfriend wasn't around, eating in secret, and then brushing my teeth and hiding the evidence. He was a health food nut and would scold me for eating sweets. Finally at age 21, I found the courage to tell him it was over. He played the same old song. I stayed strong. I moved on.

I joined Weight Watchers. I lost weight. My family told me I was too skinny. All I kept thinking was "Screw you ex-boyfriend, I am strong enough, I can be perfect … see???" However, the dieting never worked. I continued to yo-yo my way through diet after diet. Every time I ate something I considered "bad" or "not part of the plan", or if I fell of the wagon and gained the weight back I would beat myself up. Those words from that teenage boy would resurface. I would binge. I would feel guilt. I would vow to be stronger. The cycle would start again.

In 2014 a dietician I was seeing asked me if I had ever been diagnosed with a binge eating disorder. I thought "What?!? Of course not! I am a strong independent woman. I am a wife, a mother. I have a very successful and rewarding career. Certainly I could control something as simple as what I put in my mouth! I just need to be stronger. I just need to be better." However, after thinking about it for a couple of days I decided to move forward with her suggestion that I seek some group therapy. After being assessed (I thought for sure they would say I didn't belong here) I was diagnosed with a Binge Eating Disorder and accepted for therapy. My initial thought was shame. How did I allow this to happen? Why am I not strong enough?

The biggest thing I learned in group therapy is that diets don't work. If you eat a well-rounded healthy diet which includes indulgences, and get out and get some simple exercise, your body will go where it is naturally meant to be! I had to wrap my head around the fact that I will never be a size 8. I will never have a flat belly. I was uncertain about giving up my fat-free and low-cal foods. I was afraid I would gain even more weight. But I embraced this new knowledge and did the homework. I ate pasta. I ate 2% yogurt! I ate ice cream. I ate healthy foods on a regular basis. I ate regular meals. I gave up fat-free and low-cal foods and traded them in for regular fat foods. I did it in front of people. I didn't hide. It wasn't easy. It was really hard at first. There was anger. Lots of tears were shed. Many times I wanted to give up … but then something wonderful happened. I realized I was binging less and less and the negative voices were harder to hear.

It's been one year since my group ended. I still sometimes wish I was a size 8 and had a flat belly. I am still learning to love my body as it is. I have had stressful moments and have caught myself in a binge, letting old voices and words back in my head. I don't consider myself 100% recovered. It is a constant work in progress. I still sometimes want to comfort myself with food when I feel stressed and overwhelmed. But I have tools now that help. I have self-worth. I am strong. I am good enough. I am free. Will I slip up? Probably. But that's OK. I'm not perfect.

Julie: What I Wanted for My Pictures

I am most at peace by the water. We have a boat and I love being out at the beach or on the lake. The picture I would like is a woman with her arms outstretched, face tipped to the sun, wind blowing in her air, standing on a beach somewhere soaking in the warmth of the sun ... a symbol of being freed. That is me!

An Artist's Perspective: A Note from Sharon

For Julie it was obvious I had to draw a person with her face to the wind, taking in her new-found freedom from an eating disorder. The second picture contains shells on a beach, moving with the tide and being in rhythm with the universe; displaying their beauty for all to see. Just like Julie who can now appreciate her inner beauty and strengths.

Recovery Theme 11

CELEBRATING THE THINGS YOU ARE DOING RIGHT AND THE PLEASURES THAT COME FROM CHANGE

A Therapist's Perspective on Celebrating the Things that You Are Doing Right and the Pleasures that Come from Change: Michèle

Recovery is hard work and only rarely do things go smoothly. After a week (or weeks!) of doing well, you may run into a time when you feel uncertain, unhappy and your symptoms flare up. Even in a good week, there is almost always something that could have gone better—some way you could have tried harder. If you are a person who has developed an eating disorder, there is a good chance that you are also a person who focuses more on what you *didn't* do, or *haven't* accomplished than what you have done well. Every time you do something right, you see yourself building the tower of success. Every time you make a mistake, the tower is knocked down and you have to start all over again.

When you are in the early (and sometimes middle) stages of the hard work of recovery, there can be as many bad days as there are good. Certainly, there are a lot of both. I like to encourage people to stop building a tower of good days in their minds, and instead begin to build a village. If you have a bad day, well, you don't build a hut that day. But the rest of the village stands. You are much more likely to recover if you tell the part of you that is cracking the whip and barking out criticisms that you are taking a different approach. From now on, you plan to treat yourself with the same compassion and respect with which you would treat another person in the same situation. You will NOT berate yourself, and you will NOT call yourself names. Instead, just as you would for another person, you will give yourself credit for your efforts and acknowledge the factors that contribute to a day that doesn't go well. And you will celebrate your successes: You will savor the freedom of being able to join others in eating a "normal" meal; you will relish the thrill of having made it through a difficult time without binge eating; you will delight in the joy of feeling that maybe you and your body are actually good enough. The changes you make as you work to get over your eating disorder are not easy, but it is through these changes that you begin to experience the pleasure of recovery.

A Patient's Perspective on Celebrating the Things that You Do Right and the Pleasures that Come from Change:
Rachel

I don't want to alarm you, but I'm kind of low-key celebrating all the time now.

Joy used to seem like something to be experienced with caution and compensation. But I sort of decided I had to accept joy if I wanted to take a real run at recovery, or else I'd be leaving something out of the account, and I didn't like the sound of that.

Yesterday someone overheard me singing "Food makes me so very happy!" to the dinner I'd just made, in pride and anticipation. My celebration isn't always so overt and silly but I can't help but still be amazed at how different my experience is. It used to frustrate me when people said that in recovery, you might still have old thoughts or pain or shame—what was the point then! The point is this: it's totally different. At my worst now, overwhelmed or hurting, I think, "Okay, I'm overwhelmed and hurting. It makes sense and it's not forever. What do I need?" I'm still connected, and I'm still safe. And I built this difference, one brick at a time. And that still amazes me and I quietly celebrate it. And sometimes I sing to my dinner when I think no-one can hear me.

Rachel: My Recovery Story

DIAGNOSIS: BULIMIA NERVOSA

I like trees.

There was a long time when I had so much buzzing around inside my head that it felt like I couldn't settle safely on anything. It felt like there was no ground to land on, and I could only stay stirred up in thoughts that all tangled me further, none of them solid or safe. In the midst of that fragility, it felt like inside me there were emotional monsters that were constantly threatening to come screaming out to terrorize me if I couldn't keep them hidden. I felt trapped.

The worst of that particular experience wasn't when I was at my sickest. It was when I was trying to get better. When I was sick, I could sometimes just "land" on all manner of fearful, eating disordered or otherwise self-sabotaging thought—self-hatred, for instance—and I could quiet the monsters with the actions and beliefs that went with those thoughts. They felt true—truer than anything else, actually. But then, it got to the point where I couldn't fully believe in those things—they either didn't seem true or I knew that I had to start doubting them if I was going to ever recover. And once I doubted them, now I was fragile again, and had nowhere to land.

I didn't think of it this way until the day that I found a place to land—one little, insignificant, uncomplicated, personal truth. It was the dumbest thought. It was so simple. But it was true. No argument. No uncertainty. No tangle, no overwhelm, it was this:

I like trees.

A good friend and I were on a bus on a highway through Northern Ontario. I was in an intense period, a recovery crossroads, and she asked me a question about what I was going to do and I felt paralysed. I stared out the window. I felt confident in nothing at all, and I started to feel like I was floundering inside my head. I couldn't come up with an answer to her question—worse, in rising distress, I felt I couldn't come up with anything. I didn't feel solid anywhere because everything was complicated by the eating disordered and self-sabotaging framework, and by my desperate ambivalence about freeing myself from it. There was so much fear. I remember trying thoughts on, looking for anything reliable or true—could I find internal solidity in my desire to recover? No, I was still torn about it. In my goals? No, I doubted what I wanted and what I could do. In something about my music? No, I doubted my musicianship and my worthiness. My relationships? No, I instantly was in a bramble of negative beliefs about my effects on the people around me. My philosophies, my beliefs about the world itself? In that state, I doubted all of it. Nothing felt like I could count on it. I really felt like I was skidding inside my head. I looked out the window at the landscape moving past. I said, *I like trees.*

I think my friend said nothing in response to to my non sequitur and I said it again, testing it, standing on it: *I like trees.*

"I like trees" didn't save me or map out my recovery. It didn't parse the older beliefs that I used to rely on. It didn't teach me distress tolerance or fix my body image or teach me to tolerate normal eating—I needed other kinds of help, learning and persistence for that. What it did was give me an experience of feeling like there was something inside to rely on when I felt like I had nothing. I've come to believe that there is a core of me that makes sense, that's more "fundamental" than my eating disorder or my history or any of my other fears and struggles. It's that core that connects with music and knows I like trees and it's from that core that I built myself outward. I think there's a core to everyone and that the more we can believe in and connect with that, the less vulnerable we are to other things that seductively offer themselves as "reliable" and "true".

I've managed to teach myself that it is good and safe for me to be in the world, for all of its hurt and unknowns and all the magnitude of my feelings. Now, there are plenty of times when I can come up with other things that are as reliable to me as the fact that trees exist and I like the— today as I write, I feel grounded by my trust in many of my important relationships, goals, and values. That's a result of the changes of recovery and it creates a lush life for me of things I feel connected to.

And yet, I still derive a kind of solace from the fact that I know that even if I took all of that away and was in a place of huge doubt, I could build it all up again from something. I like trees. I call it a "fundamental truth". Underneath everything else there are truths I can trust. For me, that was what "I like trees" was the beginning of. It helped me.

For a long time I used to occasionally list "fundamental truths" when I felt I needed to centre myself, like I was at risk of being swept away into that groundless and overwhelmed state of mind, and the negative solutions of old habits. Connecting with what feels true to me in a given moment would help me figure out what I'm about, and that helps me a lot. I don't use "I like trees" for that anymore, really, but I do think of trees as a reminder to me that even great pain probably won't destroy me past a certain core, and that there are things I trust. And my own recovery and resilience is one of those things: with time, support, nourishment, persistence, and something to stand on, I built a strong and fortified wellness with deep and trustworthy roots, and beautiful boughs, and unknown heights.

Rachel: What I Wanted from My Pictures

I like the idea of exposed roots, like a cross-section/view where you can see the underground roots of one or more trees, plus the tree trunk part and going up into the sky, maybe with creatures in the various parts.

An Artist's Perspective: A Note from Sharon

Rachel's story made me think of trees a little differently. Ultimately I drew two pictures of trees for the significance they have in her life, and more importantly, how she is now able to visualize her wellness built on trustworthy roots, and large boughs, reaching for the limitless sky.

Recovery Theme 12

FINDING YOUR PLACE IN THE WORLD

A Therapist's Perspective on Finding Your Place in the World: Michèle

Perhaps you are someone who, in contemplating recovery, has wondered who you will be without your eating disorder. Especially if you have had your disorder for many years, it is hard to imagine a life that is not centred on restricting your food, binge eating, purging or a preoccupation with your weight and shape. What if, when these symptoms are all gone, you have nothing? How can you be sure after all your efforts to recover, that you will have a life you feel is worth living?

Many years ago, when I was still in training, my clinical supervisor commented that an eating disorder takes up so *much* of a person's energy. Because of this, it can be hard for others to see the person they once knew and loved. It can be hard for the person with the eating disorder to remember who they might be. With recovery, my supervisor said, that energy is freed up and it can be like watching a flower blossom. Recovery is often the start of developing an awareness of, and exploring your own interests. Self-awareness often starts as you attend to your own experience of eating, perhaps with observations as simple as recognizing that adding peanut butter to your breakfast leaves you less hungry by lunch time. Self-awareness about your internal experience often quickly moves from food to a better awareness of your emotional experience. For the first time, you may be trying to figure out your *own* preferences, rather than trying to make the right choice in other people's eyes. This part of recovery does not need to be frightening; it is often experienced as an exciting time of self-discovery. I have known a few people throughout the years who told me that during this time, they started a new journal and titled it something like: "Discovering who I am". Trust that when you are ready—when you reach that point in your own recovery—you will find the energy and interest to explore who you are. In that process, you will blossom; you will find your place in the world.

A Patient's Perspective on
Finding Your Place in the World:
Rex

I spent the first 25 years of my life trying to be another person. Inside, I knew I was transgender, but I didn't think that was something I was allowed to be. I thought that if I just tried hard enough, I could be "normal". I was like a puzzle piece trying to fit into the wrong puzzle. Eventually, I transitioned, and suddenly my puzzle piece fit. I learned that in order to find my place in the world, I had to be honest about who I was. Once I started to do that, I finally started living.

Sharon

It is so important that each and every one of us, realizes the gifts we possess and what we have to offer. I now believe that we need to get rid of idealized versions of what it means to be good. We all have visions of the good mother, the good student, etc. But what is more important is that we look at our own intrinsic worth, and realize that we are indeed good, valued and have innate worth. By doing just this, I have come to realize that I am "good enough" and by doing so I have found my place in the world, along with other members of my human tribe.

Rex: My Recovery Story

DIAGNOSIS: ANOREXIA NERVOSA, BINGE EATING/PURGING TYPE

I told myself I was never going to get better. I had been struggling for 10 years, going back and forth, building a life for myself and then destroying it when I relapsed. For almost every important memory I had, I could also clearly recall whether I was restricting at the time. Food had achieved some sort of romanticized, mythical status in my life—it was the only thing that mattered. Whenever things got hard, I would flee from the stress of it all and shrink my world down to input/output, gain/loss. I honestly didn't think I'd ever learn to live without it.

I never stopped seeking treatment over those 10 years, and I recovered several times, but I couldn't figure out how to make recovery last. It always felt like a Band-Aid. I'd get myself healthy for a short time, and even enjoy it. But I never felt adequate enough in recovery. When I was defying my body and losing weight, I felt a feeling of accomplishment that I couldn't find anywhere else. If I didn't feel that accomplishment I thought I was worthless as a human being. My anxiety would rise, and the only thing that would stop it would be to turn back to the eating disorder.

But here's the thing—in the bigger world, accomplishment is kind of fuzzier, harder to pin down. Accomplishment through weight loss is so tangible. You can step on the scale and see your progress. You can lose yourself in numbers. Accomplishment outside of the eating disorder takes longer and is less concrete, and it's hard to be patient.

Eventually I realized that I needed to let myself find accomplishment in other things. It was like a movie that suddenly changed from black and white into colour. Accomplishment through an eating disorder felt really good and really strong, but when I opened up my life, there were so many other ways to succeed, and such a broad range of feeling. Once I finally let myself feel that, I knew I didn't really want to go back. It's still a struggle, because I know that I can quickly solve this anxiety problem by restricting, but I don't want to go back to black and white.

This need for accomplishment is still a large part of me. Early in recovery I thought that I would have to change that in order to succeed. That tripped me up a lot, because it's a core part of who I am. I don't think I can change that, and I would feel defeated and think the eating disorder was my only option. Instead, I have spent the last two years learning how to take care of that part of me, to use it to my advantage. It's like building a tower—I have to do it slowly and carefully, but each block I get solidly in place works as a foundation for the next one, and eventually I realize I've built a taller tower than I ever did with an eating disorder. I've let myself relax, I've found things I love and have included them in my life. When I start getting anxious about what I've accomplished, I turn to these other things and practice them instead. It sounds simple, but it's not. I still need to constantly remind myself that there are other things I can accomplish. I need to keep reminding myself that accomplishment takes work and time. I am always, sometimes painfully aware that I could spend the rest of my life being really accomplished at anorexia, but to be honest, that would probably be a much shorter, much less happy, lonely existence.

Every day I get up and choose to live in colour instead of black and white. And my reward is that my life is bigger. There are more people in it. There are extremely satisfying moments. There are dreams and fears and laughter and music, but most importantly, I feel like I am finally living.

Body image was another big struggle for me. I am a transgender man, and I grew up constantly fighting the female body I was born in. And even when I did begin transition and started feeling more comfortable with who I was presenting to the world, I knew that my body wouldn't look the same as a body that was born male. At first, this made me feel extremely inadequate. This merged with my eating disorder and I had yet another reason to be thin, because to me it was the easiest way to eradicate any lingering femininity. It was another situation where I thought I would need to change myself in order to be "right". What was important for me here was time. The more time I gave myself, the farther down the path of transition I went, the more I learned about who I really was. My definition of myself changed greatly once I came out and started transitioning, and with every month that passed I learned more about who I really was deep inside. And as I finally made friends and gained courage to go back to things I loved, like theatre, I realized that what I originally thought was two options—man or woman—was actually somewhat of a spectrum. Just because I knew I was a man didn't mean that I had to force myself to be the most masculine man I could think of. So I spent a lot of time experimenting to find what I liked, disliked, wanted, cared about, and stopped trying to be what I thought others expected. It was time to get to know myself.

Really, really being honest with myself and trying to be completely true to my identity fit right in to recovery. As I struggled to figure out who I was and how to define myself, I learned a lot about how I think and feel. It made me much more self-aware and gave me tools to actually identify what kept me relapsing. Learning how to define yourself is a huge undertaking. I would advise anyone trying to know themselves to follow their gut. Do it gently and as openly as possible, you don't have to fit into anyone else's box.

This process of self-discovery changed my life. Interpersonally, I am much more comfortable because I actually know who I am now. And dare I say it? I love myself. I know I have worth and I'm eager to actually be a part of the world, where before all of this, I just wanted to hide from it.

I never thought I'd get to this point. It took a long time. But finally, I consider myself recovered. I don't think I could squeeze myself back into that tiny life again—and the beautiful thing is that I don't even want to.

Rex: What I Wanted for My Pictures

As for pictures, some things I find soothing are animals (especially cats) and nature …

An Artist's Perspective: A Note from Sharon

Upon reading Rex's story, I kept returning to images of transformation that exist in myths, legends and current popular culture. Considering Rex's journey, I settled on the phoenix and the butterfly for the artwork. The phoenix speaks to the strength needed to escape the fire, and being reborn to a new life and identity. The butterfly, so beautiful to behold, undergoes many changes (metamorphosis) and, much like Rex's life story, reminds us that we all flourish when conditions are right.

Sharon: My Recovery Story

DIAGNOSIS: BINGE EATING DISORDER

No one ever starts out thinking their irregular and poor eating habits will develop into an eating disorder. Having low self-esteem and unresolved grief in my teens made me a perfect candidate for developing an eating disorder. In grade school I was teased for being extremely skinny, but that changed almost overnight, as I became a teen and filled out. When, attending high school, like so many other teenagers, my life revolved around being accepted by the in-crowd. Much to my dismay, around them, I never felt "attractive enough", "thin enough" or "good enough". Negative comments made about my ethnicity and socioeconomic status, fueled my already firmly established perfectionistic behaviour. Although I was a normal or slightly below average weight for my height, I never felt thin enough. Wallis Simpson, the American heiress for whom King Edward abdicated the British throne, coined the phrase "you can never be too rich or too thin." Taking her lead, I was determined, even if I wasn't born with a silver spoon in my mouth, to control my weight. I succeeded for years, dieting, binge eating, exercising, starving and even tried the laxative route. Weighing myself a few times a day, I would fall into despair, even if the scale only moved by one pound. During my twenties and thirties, I would exercise for hours, despite having severe anemia to the point of exhaustion.

As months became years, and years became decades, I realized, I was technically a binge eater and eating was my coping strategy to deal with life stressors. There was no denying, it had a strong emotional component. I ate when sad, ate when glad, and ate to essentially comfort myself, so not to burden anyone with my troubles. When I would come home from work, I would eat bowls of cereal, till I finished the whole box, and then move on to whatever else I could inhale, till I felt physically ill. Wolfing down cereal or eating cookies was far more satisfying than dealing with interpersonal issues and job frustration. Surprisingly, there was actually a time when I cultivated a healthy relationship with food; trying to experiment, searching feverously for new recipes and using my friends as guinea pigs, but that soon came to an end. I fell back into my old habits. Unable to control my bingeing, food had obtained an enemy status. I could no longer keep up my exercise regime to burn off all those excess calories I was consuming. My day to day existence revolved around going on the latest and greatest new fad diet followed by weight loss, only to gain it back months later. I was the classic yo-yo dieter whose weight was continuing to climb into unhealthy regions. Common sense dictated I needed to get off this merry-go-round, but how?

I was thrilled when accepted into the program. The program allowed me to examine critically distorted thoughts about myself, and to set realistic expectations. I learned the value of meal planning, and although it can be tedious at times – it is this very planning that stopped my binge eating. The program taught me food is not the enemy and that I don't have to deny myself anything. I now view myself through an accepting and compassionate lens. It has not been easy to rewrite so many negative tapes that have been my accompanying background noise. I no longer hide cookies, and it is amazing how long they last in the house. But it has been worth it. Finally, after decades, I can say that I am comfortable being who I am and how I look. I don't feel I have to please anyone just to be accepted, although that has been a challenge my whole life. I will always have to be vigilant about my meal planning, how I handle stress, but that is a small price for this newfound sense of freedom.

A Note from Sharon about Her Own Pictures

My images are all about mindfulness and my love of doodling. When I need to focus on what is important to me, I doodle and it stops me from taking up old habits like emotional eating. What is drawn is not so important as the process and the flow I experienced when creating the doodles.

Recovery Theme 13

DISCOVERING THERE ARE MANY OPPORTUNITIES FOR YOU TO GROW

A Therapist's Perspective on Discovering There Are Many Opportunities for You to Grow: Michèle

People who come for treatment of their eating disorder are often bright, capable and accomplished in many areas of their lives. You may have started treatment of your eating disorder already knowledgeable about topics related to recovery—health, nutrition, physical activity, and emotional well-being. Ideally, recovery offers many opportunities for you to add to your knowledge and to your wisdom.

The opportunities for growth start the moment you decide to begin the work of overcoming your eating disorder. To recover, you *must* grow in self-understanding. You will come to understand your body and learn what it is to live in harmony (instead of hostility) with your biological self. You will develop a deeper understanding of your emotions through self-awareness, and acquire confidence in your ability to respond effectively to your emotions. You will learn what it takes to stop "actively hating yourself" and so create the opportunity for better body image and better self-esteem. The opportunities for growth do not end as you reach wellness; quite the opposite! Without the distraction of your eating disorder, the interests that define you as a unique person will re-emerge. Once you achieve wellness, you will have such energy to put towards these interests! The growth that follows recovery is quite wonderful to behold.

A Patient's Perspective on
Discovering There Are Many Opportunities for You to Grow:
Arnita

Often in my life, I have felt 'stuck' and unable to grow. For me, fear of change keeps me from looking for opportunities to grow. I have to be brave because the changes that I fear are often the stepping stones toward positive growth. Sometimes growing is a matter of trying, trying again, and trying differently. When I learn a new skill in one area of my life, I consider if practicing this skill in another area of my life will help me experience growth or change. And then comes the work—the trying, trying again, and trying differently.

Hannah

Through recovery I found love I never thought was there, love for others and myself. Recovery meant making my life into one in which I could thrive, and I am thriving.

Arnita: My Recovery Story

DIAGNOSIS: BINGE EATING DISORDER

Life was chaotic, confusing, overwhelming.

Throughout my childhood, I experienced abuse and neglect. As a result, I developed separate personalities to help me cope with my experiences. Having learned how to split and dissociate, whenever I was faced with new trauma I simply developed a new personality. This process wasn't intentional; I wasn't even aware what was going on. I was in my early forties before being diagnosed with dissociative identity disorder (DID).

Learning about the personalities, listening to their stories, and exploring how to function as a whole and healthy person has been a challenge. With counselling and support, I've learned how to live in a way that addresses the needs of each personality. Everyone deserves the opportunity to recover from being a victim, to be heard and respected, and to develop skills as a survivor.

Food has always been very complicated for me. In my family, food was used to reward, punish, and control. There were occasions that our family didn't have enough food. At other times, I was forced to finish what was on my plate and/or eat food that I didn't like.

Creeping out of my bed in the middle of the night to forage for snacks was commonplace. Stealing money from my siblings' piggy banks enabled me to buy treats at the variety store. To soothe myself, I ate normally in front of others and then binged in private.

Being of a stocky build, I was teased unmercifully by my peers and my family. In my teens, I began to experiment with dieting, fasting, and over-exercising. Despite all attempts, I gained more weight and began to believe that I deserved all the harsh opinions presented by the media, friends, and family.

As an adult, food continued to be difficult. I either pretended that I didn't care about my health and appearance and ate with no sense of control or I continued the cycle of dieting and over-exercising. I rarely felt that I was in control of my decisions.

Life was chaotic, confusing, overwhelming.

Several years ago, I attended an information session at the Eating Disorders Clinic to support a friend who was involved in the Binge Eating program. During the information session, I realized that I needed the help my friend was receiving and that I desperately wanted to be accepted to the program.

During the intake process for the Eating Disorder Clinic, I agonized as to whether I should disclose my diagnosis of DID. I didn't want to be excluded from the program! However, I didn't know how treatment would work with different personalities who all have a separate approach to food, eating, and wellness. Having decided that full disclosure is the best, I let the team know of my situation and was accepted to the Making Changes class.

The first several weeks of Making Changes, I experienced a wonderful sense of relief. I met others who also have binge eating disorder. We speak the same language. We understand how it feels to want to stop eating and then eat, and eat, and eat. The information and education were encouraging. The class leaders were compassionate and understanding.

I was ready to make changes!

Except, I have multiple personalities and not all the personalities agreed to take this class. Some didn't want to change. Change is scary—and hard. I began to feel that I was in the wrong place at the wrong time and for all the wrong reasons.

For me, one of the biggest steps forward was to acknowledge that it took me a lifetime to get to where I am, and it was going to take time to learn new habits and patterns. I realized that I needed to trust the treatment plan. These were choices I could make. I did have control of my decisions.

Another challenge was to let go of my need to do everything perfectly. I don't have to do this exactly right every day and every time. I can make a mistake, let go of it, and move forward. I can have a difficult day where I feel like I'm not doing well, and still choose to do well.

I believe I am well on my way to recovery. I think of my recovery as a work in progress. I'm further along than I was at the end of the Making Changes class and further along than I was a month ago. I don't compare my recovery to others' recovery. They have their progress—I have mine.

I no longer binge eat. I continue to work daily on making wise food choices. I find it helpful to record my meals. Sometimes, I eat mechanically so that I eat often enough. These tools help me to avoid binging.

The Body Image class helped me to accept my body. I'm quite proud of my body. It has survived not only the abuse and neglect of my childhood but the effects of my binge eating. Now, I dress differently. I walk differently. I live differently.

Life can be chaotic, confusing, and overwhelming and I have the skills and tools to live as a whole and healthy person. I love this new life of freedom and hope!

Arnita: What I Wanted for My Pictures

I wonder if the artist could use the bird-feeding idea for my picture.
I find the act of feeding the birds calming, exciting, and instructive.
I'm amazed at the courage of the birds.
The birds are, by their nature, constantly mindful.
They are mindful of the danger and confident in their skill to deal with the danger.
They are mindful of their task—get food, eat it, come back for the appropriate amount, repeat as needed.
They are opportunistic. As soon as people arrive with food, they begin to investigate.
They are not foolhardy. At the smallest movement of my hand, they are gone.
(One could almost believe that they have been to a well-led DBT class).

An Artist's Perspective: A Note from Sharon

I was so touched by Arnita's request to include chickadees, which reinforced my belief about the healing power of all different kinds of animals. Chickadees have an amazing ability to adapt to cold temperatures, which can serve as a symbol for all of us. Like the chickadee, Arnita, has adapted despite her very difficult beginnings to embrace a healthier lifestyle.

Hannah: My Recovery Story

DIAGNOSIS: ANOREXIA NERVOSA, BINGE-EATING/PURGING TYPE

I never would have guessed that I would battle an eating disorder.

I became sick during high school. I had always played high-level sports, I was strong, healthy and far from overweight. I never thought twice about calories or experienced dissatisfaction with my body. I remember weighing myself for the first time in a long time and being surprised at the number on the scale, not upset, simply surprised. The plan was never to lose weight; I just wanted to eat in a more mindful way.

Before I knew it I began cutting out different foods, compulsively exercising, and constantly checking my weight. My obsession became worse and worse. I was eventually diagnosed with Anorexia Nervosa, Binge/Purge Type. I lost a lot of weight, but more frightening than that I lost out on significant parts of life. My illness kept me from experiencing all the amazing things that this world has to offer. I denied my body what it needed, I distanced myself from my friends and my family, I was too tired to do the things I once loved, I lost all motivation. Mentally I was miserable, and slowly my body began to deteriorate as well. I realized that I did not want to live this way anymore.

Recovery was the most difficult thing I have ever done. My recovery began with the St. Joseph's Eating Disorders clinic and I owe so much to the amazing team of people who helped me through.

The most difficult part of my recovery was the beginning. First I had to accept that I was sick and that I needed help, which was extremely challenging. Next I had to trust what these doctors were telling me; that recovery is worth it, that I needed to include 'treats' in my diet (treats?!?!). It meant facing the root of my illness, the fears and beliefs I had long buried away. I had to reintroduce the foods I had brainwashed myself into believing were forbidden. Even harder than eating these foods was realizing that I actually wanted to eat them; I felt like a failure. Slowly, things began to get easier and easier. There was a small phase in the middle of my recovery where it was tempting to stop. I thought to myself, "I'm comfortable here, look at all the work I've done. This is enough." But it was a trick. Believe that you are stronger than your illness, and that above all **you deserve recovery**. The last stage of my journey was bittersweet. On the one hand my body had changed and I hadn't completely come to terms with it. I doubted my decision to recover whenever the negative thoughts found their way back into my head. But then I began to really experience things the way I should have been all along; I laughed more, I enjoyed eating, I reconnected with those I loved and was once more able to do what I loved. I let go of the perpetual anxiety and guilt, and regained my sense of self-worth.

I have been 'recovered' for nearly two years; I say 'recovered' because I believe recovery is something of a spectrum. I was weight restored and no longer allowed my illness to dictate my life but I was not fully recovered; I still struggled to accept where I was. I began revaluating what in my life I truly valued and removing all the things I didn't. I decided to finally believe for myself that I am more than my body. I removed people and things that were a negative impact on my mental health; damaging social media accounts, destructive people. I sat down and made a list of all the things I truly wanted to do, all of which happened to be achievable regardless of my

appearance. I came up with a mantra, and repeated it to myself any time I felt my illness trying to fight its way back. Know that "I am" truly are the two most powerful words you can say because whatever follows becomes your reality.

I have been **fully** recovered for almost a year and I do believe that full recovery is possible. My eating disorder is a part of me, just like all the experiences we go through in our lives. It helped shape who I am today, but it is no longer an active part of my life. It is a reminder of how far I've come and how strong I am. There will definitely bad days, days you don't want to get out of bed, days you wonder if it's worth the fight, but I promise you it is. Know that you have already conquered every one of your bad days. You can keep going.

I look back on where I was compared to where I am now and I am so grateful. Grateful for all of the help and support I had along the way. Grateful for my body and all of the amazing things it does for me. Through recovery I found love I never thought was there, love for others and myself. Recovery meant making my life into one in which I could thrive, and I am thriving. **Recovery is worth it.**

I am a whole
I am a soul with a body, and if you watch, I will bloom

Hannah: What I Wanted for My Pictures

I was thinking, for the illustration, a tall sunflower …

An Artist's Perspective: A Note from Sharon

I was thrilled that Hannah chose sunflowers. Their beautiful golden faces always point to the life-giving rays of the sun. Hannah's words " I am a whole / I am a soul with a body, and if you watch, I will bloom" are certainly relevant to the image of the sunflower, for one of its meanings is related to nourishing yourself in all domains.

Recovery Theme 14

FEELING THAT YOU ARE IN CHARGE

A Therapist's Perspective on Feeling that You Are in Charge: Michèle

Years ago I worked with a teenager who had developed anorexia in elementary school. I met her as she was transitioning to high school, and by that point she had already had years of therapy, and numerous hospitalizations. At first, she wasn't able to make changes to her eating and activity, and we eventually made the decision that she needed, yet again, another hospitalization. I remember telling her as she prepared for admission that, even in hospital, recovery was up to her. I told her that the hospital could only rescue her temporarily. If she wanted to be well, she was going to need to realize that she was the one in charge. The first part of her hospitalization did not go particularly well, and then suddenly, things changed. She told me that she'd realized during her admission that the hospital couldn't made her better; that she was the only one who could do this. She needed to be in charge. This was the beginning of her recovery.

Perhaps you worry that in coming for treatment you are not doing recovery yourself; you are taking the easy route in letting others help you. The reality is that, no matter what treatment you receive for your eating disorder—whether in or out of the hospital, once a week or every day— you will not recover unless you feel like you are in charge. You may be very scared and uncertain of yourself at first. In therapy, if you work hard to meet the goals you set each week, your confidence in yourself will grow. You will come to know that you have the ability to face your fears; that you are in charge, not your eating disorder. After you realize this, there will be no stopping you. The only person responsible for your recovery is you.

A Patient's Perspective on Feeling that You Are in Charge:
Sheryl

During program while trying to regulate my eating (which was daunting enough), I was also hit with the breakdown of a romantic relationship followed shortly by the death of a beloved pet. I was heartbroken. There were weeks I would sit in session and be in tears. I cannot control what happens to me in life, I can only control how I respond to it. I focus on how good recovery feels. I am in charge of my recovery. Every single day.

Sylvie

Binge Eating Disorder is an illness that exploits your ability to be out of control. We taught ourselves to eat our feelings. Now … Imagine not thinking about food 24/7. Imagine eating what you need throughout the day including treats and not beating yourself up for it. Imagine accepting who you are; the curves and shape of your body—your set point weight. Imagine not being controlled by food. That's how it feels.

"I can be changed by what happens to me. But I refuse to be reduced by it." —Maya Angelou

Sheryl: My Recovery Story

DIAGNOSIS: OTHER SPECIFIED FEEDING AND EATING DISORDER—ATYPICAL ANOREXIA NERVOSA, PURGING

In 2003, at the age of 34, I remember seeing myself in the mirror in the washroom at work, and REALLY seeing myself at 260 lbs. In the past, I would try to stay focused on my face, thinking "I still look good." This time, I saw what other people saw. I was disgusted with myself. "How did I let this happen?" I used to walk the hallways of the office with my eyes trained down on the floor. If I don't look at people, they won't notice me. I tried to be invisible. Pretty difficult to hide a 260 lb body.

A coworker of mine was getting married in 2004, and wanted to lose some weight before her big day. She asked me if I would go with her to join a diet program. Over the course of a year and a half, I lost 110 lbs. to get to my goal weight of 150 lbs. I received so many compliments and people I hadn't seen in years didn't recognize me. I hadn't been this thin since I was in Grade 10. However, I wasn't happy with my goal weight. I could be thinner! Exercise now consumed my thoughts 24/7. If I went out for a meal, I'd exercise for 90 minutes to work it off. It became two hours daily, 30 km of running per week, and 5 hours of exercise on both Saturday and Sunday. I was never home. I was getting thinner and thinner, and feeling great. I had so much energy! At 130 lbs., the scale stopped moving. I hadn't had a period in a year. I would see people looking at me while I was running. I thought in my head, "They wish they looked like me!" I was obsessed with exercise. I ran in the snow, in the rain, in the humidity. I never skipped my run. Eventually my body gave out. It couldn't sustain eating only 600 calories a day and exercising the way I was. My back gave out. I had to stop running. My period returned after three weeks. The weight slowly started coming back.

In 2008 I decided to leave a marriage I was unhappy in. I waited almost four years before trying to date again. In May of 2012 at the age of 43, I went on my first date. In the course of the evening he admitted to me that he already lived with a woman. I felt so disgusted and ashamed that I went home and made myself throw up. It's the first time in my life I've ever done this. The relief I felt physically after that was incredible. I started using purging to actually control my anxiety, not for weight loss. It soon spiraled out of control. What started as maybe once every few days, became every day. Not just one meal, it eventually became every meal.

In July 2012 I met I man I really enjoyed being with. I kept my secret hidden. I never purged in his home, even though he'd cook me meals and feed me wine which were against my strict diet. I continued to purge, my eyes would hurt from the bulging, my throat would burn, my lips were dry and cracked, and I still kept going. I started vomiting anywhere, not just at home. In restaurants, in my office garbage can if there were too many people in the washroom. I'd have a party in my home, and while everyone was inside the house eating, I'd go out to the garage and purge in a garbage can there. I knew at this point I had to get this under control. After over a year of this behaviour I sought help from my family doctor. I was ready to admit I had a problem. I was referred to the program at St Joseph's Hospital.

Initially I was fearful I'd be in a room of 16-year-old girls that were anorexic. I feared being the fattest girl in the room. I remember being surprised my first session to be surrounded with people more my own age! During the course of the program, we were given a meal plan to follow. I had given up tracking my food intake over a year ago, knowing that it drove my restricting behaviours. Being told I had to start tracking again had me very fearful. I had also cut out entire food groups from my diet. Having to reintroduce them also had me terrified. I knew if I wanted to recover, I had to have faith in the program. Once I started to regulate my eating, I was gaining weight. I had been diagnosed with Crohn's disease in 2010 and found eating normally wreaked havoc with my bowels. I was unable to go to the bathroom. I thought I had a bowel constriction and went to the hospital only to be told it was constipation. I was struggling. I wanted to feel better, but my stomach wasn't processing the food. I wasn't eating all my grains. I knew they were causing my stomach issues. As I ate, the food would sit in my upper belly waiting to be purged.

I decided on December 31, 2013 that I would never purge again. I have stuck to that promise to myself. It took me a good six months of normalized eating before my stomach would digest properly. I took recovery day by day. I WANTED to get well. I've been recovered now for over two full years. Do I ever have times I over-indulge? Yes, but not often. Do I purge over it? NO. I have found other ways to cope with life. I eat healthy meals, I don't restrict, I exercise for enjoyment, not driven by compulsion. I am able to enjoy socializing again, and I can finally look in the mirror and be content with what I see. A healthy, strong body!

Sheryl: What I Wanted for My Pictures

I'd love to have something related to horses. I go riding a few times a month, and it's the one thing I look forward to more than anything.

An Artist's Perspective: A Note from Sharon

It is obvious that Sheryl loves horses so both her pictures are of horses, just content to be. Hopefully the pictures will be a reminder of her love of riding and these majestic beasts, and the importance of doing what we love.

Sylvie: My Recovery Story

DIAGNOSIS: BINGE EATING DISORDER

It always amazed me how you look at yourself through your own eyes. I've had a warped view of myself for as long as I can remember. This negative sense of self was brought on by growing up in an abusive home; having my father die when I was young; surviving being raped; plus multiple surgeries. Harsh realities to face, so I filled myself up with food to numb the pain; binged to be precise. I would spend my days fantasizing about my next meal. Part of me knew this was not normal behavior but it was my way of having control over my life ... or so I thought. The trick when eating in public was to make it appear as though you were eating reasonable portions but truth be told I had stashes of food hidden for later.

I began binge eating when I was about 20 years old. That was over half a lifetime ago. Of course it was not seen as binge eating back then. You were labeled as an over-eater and it was because you had no self-control; and I believed it. It would take me being at 305 lbs. with Type 2 diabetes and a slew of health issues before I sought help. For me that was bariatric surgery. For about 18 months after the surgery I honestly thought I was "cured". However, the disordered eating had only been abated; it would return but this time I had had the bariatric surgery; therefore binging was causing me enormous amount of physical pain and placing the bariatric process at risk.

I was fortunate to have a family doctor who listened and referred me to the BED program. I remember the first few weeks attending the program. I was sure they couldn't help me; didn't see myself sharing with the group. I was ready to quit the program. I halfheartedly did the work, especially having to write down everything I ate. It's not an "ah-ha" moment but more of a gradual awakening. I stuck with the program and I have never regretted that decision. Facing your demons is never easy. There were weeks where I would have preferred to curl myself up in a little ball and forget the world. During one of our sessions we were writing about core values, emotions and triggers. How they can clash within us. I knew for me that it would be standing up to my mother; the woman who had abused me, especially emotionally and psychologically. I felt I would never be able to do so. I wanted her to say she was sorry for what she did. Instead I learned to accept what had happened to me and move forward by focusing on my response to her. You see, "It is what it is." That became my mantra. The program taught me to accept that I will never hear those words, but more importantly, it was how I responded to not only my mother but to the world that mattered.

As much as I dreaded being in a group setting those first few weeks, they became a strength I could draw on. For me the test came when I was able to not let my mother get to me on a family visit. I pictured the group in my mind and focused on the hard work we had been doing. It was not important what was being said but the fact that I was able to say "Enough." I refused to let her words get to me. I was a grown woman who finally was able to say "Enough." Sharing that moment with the group the following week and having them support me in my response made me feel strong.

I understand that doing the work is going to be hard. However, I do hope you will stick with it, especially when it is at the hardest point for you. That point will be different for everyone, depending on your experiences. I also have learned to reach out when I feel there are days I am not

managing my recovery. Many times, I have gone back to using the food records to help me back on track. So please don't beat yourself up during the difficult moments.

One day, as I was walking towards my six-month evaluation, I ran into another person who was six weeks into the treatment program. She asked me "When did you feel cured?" —The biggest thing you will learn is to accept that you will never be "cured"; you will be in recovery and always will be. By the look on that woman's face I gathered she wasn't pleased to hear that, but I also know that if she keeps with the BED program she will learn to accept and feel healthier. Recovery to me means acceptance, truly acknowledging your existence AND accepting yourself, warts and all. Once you start seeing and feeling what YOU are truly about is when the journey to healing starts.

I accept there will be difficult days, even after almost two years, and that I will slip back into binge habits, but I have learned not to berate myself but to say "It is what it is" and make a fresh start the next day. Recovery is the journey. Recovery means it's ongoing. Recovery means acceptance. Remember that at any given moment you have the power to say, "This is not how the story is going to end."

Sylvie: What I Wanted for My Pictures

This is Jamster, my guinea pig. He is most missed. He was a lovely little creature and if they have souls then he had the best soul ever.

An Artist's Perspective: A Note from Sharon

After Sylvie send me pictures of her beloved pet, I knew, absolutely, that both pictures had to be of him. He is so adorable.

Recovery Theme 15

HAVING HOPE FOR YOUR FUTURE

A Therapist's Perspective on Having Hope for Your Future: Michèle

I have heard people say that the only way you can recover from an eating disorder is if you hit rock bottom. So what is "rock bottom"? Do you have to lose your education or your job, your interests, your friends, your partner, your family and your health before you find the motivation to recover? I think not.

In my experience, it seems to take a mixture of misery and hope for a person to want to work at recovery. You need enough misery to make you want to consider doing something different. You need enough hope to feel that the work of recovery will make your life better. I worked with a young woman whose eating disorder had cost her almost everything; the only thing she still had was a loving family determined to support her in getting better. When I first met her, her weight was so low there was no question that she would need to be hospitalized. As we prepared for her admission, we discussed her fears. As you might expect, she was afraid of what she would have to eat, afraid of giving up physical activity, and very afraid of gaining weight. However, what she was most afraid of was that she would never be able to rebuild a life for herself. I told her that it made complete sense that she would feel this way, especially as she had lost so much. I asked her to trust that with wellness would come an energy and interest in life that she could not yet imagine. Rebuilding her life might take some work, it is true, but she would feel ready when the time was right. This is exactly what happened. If you are fortunate enough to still have many good things in your life, you have good reason to hope that wellness will only make these things better. It can be harder to see what your life will look like if you have lost more to your eating disorder. Trust that the desire and the energy to rebuild your life will come naturally when you are ready; you too have every reason to have hope for your future.

A Patient's Perspective on
Having Hope for Your Future:
Megan

Before beginning my journey to better health, I felt skeptical about the future. I'm a procrastinator at the best of times and a quitter at my worst. I always convinced myself that I'd try my best and if it didn't work out then there would always be some other option, another method to regain my health and feel 'normal', whatever that is. From what I've learned this past year, I've found that setbacks are not only a given, but they are also a gift of sorts. Any setback I've faced has held the answer on how to move forward, teaching me things about myself that would later help me down the road. So don't shy away from mistakes, as they don't indicate failure. They are the building blocks you need in order to build yourself a more balanced and healthy future.

And 'normal' is only a word that society uses to describe a group of people, people who also struggle with their own insecurities and who have to deal with the added pressure of maintaining that façade of 'normalcy'. So, no matter where you turn, there are people struggling in their own way, just as you are.

Danielle

Staying hopeful—this was never easy for me.

I will never forget the day everyone came to visit me at residential treatment: parents, sisters, brother, nephew and grandparents. This moment helped me solidify my goals: I wished to survive ED no matter what because I had people in my life that I wanted to see to the end. And that is the hope that I held onto when times got really tough: I held onto that small glimmer of hope that my family life could be peaceful. I knew that if I kept fighting ED, I would attain that reality. I fought hard to keep ED in the past. So I knew I had the strength within to fight against ED.

I can remember in my early twenties, sitting with my therapist in her office and her mentioning that I was almost to a point where I was considered chronically ill; that is, I might never recover from my eating disorder (ED). Here I am though, five years symptom-free, because I did not lose hope for myself.

Megan: My Recovery Story

DIAGNOSIS: BINGE EATING DISORDER

I didn't really consider myself as someone who had a binge eating disorder until I found myself a part of a BED group. I have this very inconvenient quality where I don't realize I'm in an unfortunate situation until someone tells me I ought to work on fixing it. This often happens because I live way too much in my head, in daydreams, to the point where the real me—grounded in reality—comes as a surprise. I often find my reflection a surprise, as if I became big overnight, rather than gradually over time. I wasn't deluded; I've tried to lose weight in diet form more times than I can count on one hand and in desperate resolutions of my own making more times than I can count on *both* hands. Yet somehow, when I attended my first BED group I found myself shocked to be recognized as having an eating disorder.

According to my own preconceived notion of eating disorders, I shouldn't have one. I hadn't suffered an unpleasant childhood, I wasn't particularly sad nor was I depressed. I thought that if I had no *proper* reason to be suffering, then I couldn't be suffering, really. It seems silly to think that now, as eating disorders are just as much a product of day-to-day things like societal conventions as they are a product of past and present suffering. Since when did someone need a *good reason* to be in distress, anyway? As if there are people standing by, judging whether or not you have a *right* to be struggling; it's almost laughable.

It's a genuine worry and guilt people struggle with. However much people tell you—professionals even—that you are recognized as struggling with an eating disorder, you feel as if you have to have evidence to back it up. It's probably the thing I struggled with most at the beginning of my journey to recovery. Hearing the stories of others and how they'd found themselves in their current predicament made me feel like some sort of fraud.

The origin of this feeling revealed itself to me when we began working on core beliefs. It turns out my core belief was that I wasn't worthy of attention—of any kind—from others. This belief manifested itself in my day-to-day life without me even recognizing it for what it was. I'd always blamed it on anxiety, but even my anxiety was probably just a by-product of this belief. It kept me from allowing family or friends to get too close—I shunned hugs and compassion like the plague—and even kept me from pursuing new relationships. Even now, when faced with compassion of any form, I feel like crying. I feel exposed and vulnerable; like people can see I'm not worth their time and just patronize me with compliments and affection out of sympathy. Which I realize now is a little absurd; why would people bother with *fake* affection if they didn't have to? I know I wouldn't. When I give affection, I give it whole-heartedly and with genuine feeling behind it. If I didn't feeling anything, I wouldn't make any effort.

Working on this journey to recovery—because it is *work*—helped me in more ways than just in regulating my health. I didn't start eating mechanically, stop binging and continue on with life as if nothing had happened. The work I did in the BED group dredged up more things that needed attending to in my life along the way and I'm grateful that it did or else I feel like I'd still be walking around with them weighing me down. That was definitely a focus in the group; dealing with the root of the problem. For example, it does no good to treat a rash without finding out what caused it in the first place; otherwise it'll just come back in the future.

Moving forward, I feel like I have insights and information that will help me continue to build on the progress I've made. The progress is interesting, too. Not all work is tedious and unpleasant; you may even come to find that there are interesting things about yourself to learn and build upon. My most memorable moment of progress throughout group was finding my word. One of the compliments I've gotten most over my lifetime is that I'm 'cute'. When working on my core belief, I worked hard to flip it on its head and remind myself that I was worthy of whatever attention my friends and family chose to give me. That included allowing myself to believe I was things like 'cute'. When I allowed myself to believe it, my imagination went a little wild with it—as it does—and I left group one day imaging myself as a giant teddy bear, hugging people left and right without any second-guessing. I didn't like the word 'cute', though, as it held all the bitter feelings I had towards the idea of people patronizing me. So I tweaked it a bit. I gave myself a word to wear like a teddy suit whenever I was feeling down about myself. I started calling myself *plush*. It's hard to be angry or disappointed in yourself when you imagine yourself as a plush teddy—in my opinion, the ultimate symbol of hugs, ironically.

I'm never good at concluding things, as I tend to get all dramatic and I start making big, ridiculous overgeneralizations. That doesn't do anyone any good and life isn't about the conclusion, after all, it's about the journey. It's about moving forward and *enjoying it*. The means have to justify the end and all that good stuff. Throw away that notion that the end justifies the means; that's the dieters' way of thinking and you'll begin to see—or perhaps already do see—that it hasn't done you or anyone else any good.

An Artist's Perspective: A Note from Sharon

How better to represent something cuddly and soft than to include the ubiquitous teddy bear? Rather than drawing a group of people hugging, when I read Megan's story I definitely knew a teddy bear had to be included, and hearts for this person who loves so deeply.

Danielle: My Recovery Story

DIAGNOSIS: BULIMIA NERVOSA AND ANOREXIA NERVOSA, BINGE EATING/PURGING TYPE

I don't really know where ED started. I had a happy childhood; I am the third child of four with two very loving parents and so many good memories. There's no denying that I was a chubby child. I can remember the first time someone called me fat, I was swimming at a friends' house and we were talking about how we did not like mosquitoes. I mentioned that mosquitoes really liked me and she piped up, "Because you're fat?"

By twelve years old, I was into dieting, but never with very much success. By Grade 10 (15 years old), I was bulimic. My weight fluctuated, I weighed myself every day, I was always on a diet. There were days when I would go put on a pair of pants and they did not fit me anymore and I would just cry. I can remember going to mall with my mom and just crying in the change room as I tried on pants. I thought I was disgusting.

My parents did everything they could to help me. They found out after a few months of purging (hard not to notice the dirty toilet) and confronted me. Purging started as a way to manage my weight and it had turned into something I could not stop. ED led me to believe that I was unlikeable and not worth anyone's time. Throughout ED's existence, I pushed friends and family away thinking ED was right.

After high school, I attended university. My parents and I decided I would go into residence my first year. I thought that regular meals and snacks in that setting would help me regain my life; however, it only lasted for so long until the same thoughts returned and I fell back into ED's ways. I went back to school in the fall, into a house with six girls that I had met in student residence. It was the same story as first-year residence: first few months were good and then I relapsed because I was restricting. This time it got ugly: I stole my housemates' food, I found secret emails from them to my mother, I plugged the toilet too many times, and eventually I had to move out. I wish I could tell them I am sorry, but they no longer talk to me.

By the end of second year, I had reached a medically unsafe weight. My mom and dad knew it was time for to seek inpatient treatment. Canadian help was unavailable as quickly as American, so off I went. I had a very hard time fighting ED and being away from family. I left that treatment centre early and was smaller than when I first got there. Unfortunately, I relapsed within a few days of being home. I'll never forget my sister crying when she heard me in the bathroom. It broke my heart and yet, I couldn't stop.

Enter second treatment centre. It was time for another interruption in my ED symptoms in a controlled environment. It was a large difference to inpatient treatment in the U.S.: I was able to keep my cell phone, the public telephone was available 24/7 and most importantly, my family could visit me several times a week since it was just a vehicle drive away.

I still felt that I needed something to wake me up every morning, a reason to push forward: enter my search for a dog. The day I graduated from Homewood, we picked up Ciccio on our way home. I did not shower, leave my house, or consider ED for three days. Not only did he give me a reason to wake up in the morning, but he also showed me what unconditional love really means. After a few days, my mind took over and all I wanted was to eat everything in the kitchen. I am sure my family felt like their world was crumbling as they heard me purge upstairs, but all I could think about was getting rid of all the food I had just eaten.

After I graduated from university, I entered the working world. Unfortunately, I was unable to find anything in my field and I ended up working several part-time jobs. I needed all three jobs to afford my bulimia. My purchases from the grocery store were embarrassing; I worked a lot of hours and spent a lot of money to drown my emotions. After a few months in the workforce I was doing well in regards to my eating disorder: my symptoms had become manageable and I was eating regular meals and snacks. Then, my Nonno started not looking well and he was diagnosed with liver cancer. I did not know how to deal; I needed to void my sadness, and my need to binge and purge was not manageable. Within a month cancer had taken over his body and he left this world. ED took over again. I was unable to control who left my life, but food would never leave me. It was years before I revisited the thought of recovery.

When my boyfriend moved to California in October 2010, my ED became more of an annoyance than a help. I spent a lot of time on webcam with my boyfriend while we were long distance; there was no way I could be binging on camera with him. I wanted to spend time on camera with him more than I wanted to be with ED. I went to California to spend New Year's with him. I had to control ED for two weeks. I learned so much those two weeks living with my boyfriend and his family. His mom showed me that I did not need to constantly be working at my future; instead I could do what I was able to in that moment and let the world manage the rest. She showed me what it was like to eat a regular meals and snacks, and be okay with it.

In May 2011, I went to see my boyfriend in California again. When I returned home, I came home with determination to recover. I wanted an ED-free life and family with my boyfriend. I needed to put everything I had learned in treatment into play. Eating all my snacks and meals in California really helped when I got back home. During this recovery attempt, each time I relapsed I took it as a learning experience, an opportunity to prevent that from happening again, rather than catastrophizing and thinking I would never get better. I was not going to give up. Recovery took a lot of patience, fighting my mind and learning about body cues, all skills I lost when I was living with ED. After a few ED symptom free weeks, I remember my mom came into my bedroom and was crying and she said, "I am so happy to have my daughter back." We hugged and cried for a few minutes … it felt so good!

I am currently working on starting a bookkeeping business and developing a personal life I am proud of. ED no longer controls me, and when those voices creep into my thoughts, I immediately shut them down because I know that I am way better off without ED.

An Artist's Perspective: A Note from Sharon

Reading Danielle's story, images of water and the sun and the capacity to heal entered my mind. I could envision her standing by the water's edge, embracing nature. I created a lighthouse, for I think Danielle is now guided by her own inner strength and has found light at the end of the tunnel.

My Recovery Story

....

....

....

....

....

....

....

....

....

....

....

....

....

....

....

....

....

My Artwork